Tuscany-Canterbury

T0308264

Tuscany-Canterbury
A Baltimore Neighborhood History

EILEEN HIGHAM

MARYLAND HISTORICAL SOCIETY · BALTIMORE

© 2004 Maryland Historical Society

Library of Congress Cataloging-in-Publication Data

Higham, Eileen, 1922-
    Tuscany-Canterbury : a Baltimore neighborhood history / Eileen Higham.
        p. cm.
    Includes bibliographical references and index.
    ISBN 0-938420-77-1 (alk. paper)
    1. Tuscany-Canterbury (Baltimore, Md.)—History. 2. Baltimore (Md.)—History. I. Title.
    F189.B16T87 2004
    975.2'6—dc22   2004020512

The paper used in this publication meets the minimum requirements of the
American National Standard for Information Sciences Permanence of Paper or
Printed Library Materials
ANSI Z39.48-1984

Frontispiece: Courtyard at One Oak Place, n.d.
(The John Work Garrett Library, Johns Hopkins University.)

*This book is dedicated to the memory of John Higham,
who taught me all I know about history.*

Contents

Illustrations

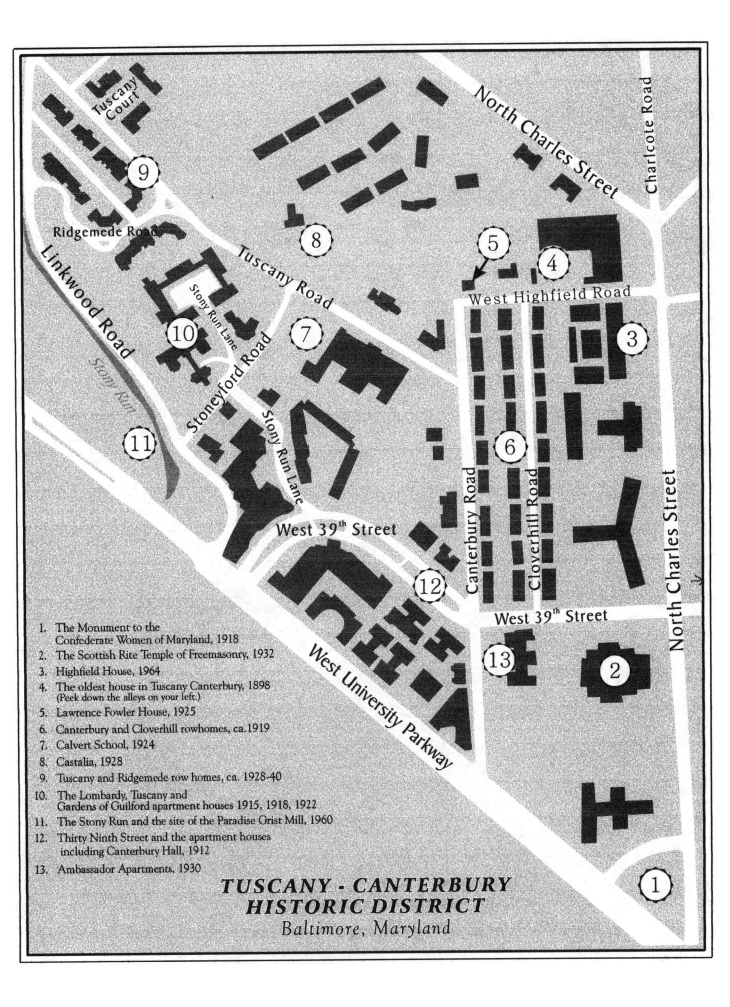

1. The Monument to the
   Confederate Women of Maryland, 1918

2. The Scottish Rite Temple of Freemasonry, 1932

3. Highfield House, 1964

4. The oldest house in Tuscany Canterbury, 1898
   (Peek down the alleys on your left.)

5. Lawrence Fowler House, 1925

6. Canterbury and Cloverhill rowhomes, ca.1919

7. Calvert School, 1924

8. Castalia, 1928

9. Tuscany and Ridgemede row homes, ca. 1928-40

10. The Lombardy, Tuscany and
    Gardens of Guilford apartment houses 1915, 1918, 1922

11. The Stony Run and the site of the Paradise Grist Mill, 1960

12. Thirty Ninth Street and the apartment houses
    including Canterbury Hall, 1912

13. Ambassador Apartments, 1930

TUSCANY - CANTERBURY
HISTORIC DISTRICT
Baltimore, Maryland

Preface

Several years ago I found myself in a state of enforced leisure, occasioned by changes in the structure of my career of fifty years, and physical limitations. Casting about for a diversion, and examining what I truly liked, living in this neighborhood was surely one item. There is no place I would rather live in the entire United States, much as I enjoy many other places.

No one had written a history of this community. Being married to a historian tends to turn one's mind to history. I start at the very beginning, when this was nothing but wilderness, belonging to pre-history. I then traced the sequence of events from the wilderness to the present, to the streets and buildings where we live today, to the small piece of the earth that 2,875 of us share with each other. I placed the various stages of growth and development within the wider social context of their occurrence and then examined the census data for this neighborhood's three available decades. Finally, I obtained accounts from long-time residents whose stories and memories enrich this chronicle with their experiences of living here, in Tuscany-Canterbury.

To accomplish the task I laid out, I consulted the many resources available in Baltimore City and Baltimore County (for we were once part of the county), both printed material and information obtained from literally dozens of people. Neither I nor anyone else could have obtained the information in this story, even if working for a lifetime, without tapping the knowledge and memories of many people, as well as reading published material. For this is not a history of elections and battles, or of other public events that are easily accessible. It is a history of a community and those who planned it.

I have recorded the sources of my indebtedness in the Acknowledgments and in the Bibliographical Note at the end of the book. Thus, what began as a search for a diversion became a passionate interest of three years and more. Some might call this work; I call it pleasure, and, indeed, I have written it entirely for my own pleasure. It is not a scholarly work, but rather an affectionate history rooted in fact, insofar as fact can be obtained.

Building the Ambassador, view from Canterbury Road and University Parkway, n.d. (Maryland Historical Society.)

Acknowledgments

The many people and organizations who so kindly answered my questions included friends and neighbors, architects, realtors, builders, librarians, journalists, authors, archivists, city and county government agencies, and professional organizations.

Three informants deserve special mention. John McGrain of the Baltimore County Planning Office provided facts and pictures from his vast store of personal resources, information I could not have found on my own. His generosity to a person totally unknown to him was extraordinary. Mary Ellen Hayward, architectural historian and author, with Charles Belfoure, of The Baltimore Row House, (New York: Princeton Architectural Press, 1999) shared obscure items of information, made many useful suggestions, and introduced me to the complexities of the Circuit Court for Baltimore City Land Records Office. Dean Wagner, a fellow neighborhood aficionado, shared his research on John Ahlers, the architect whose work is prominent in Northwood and in Tuscany-Canterbury. He also offered esoteric items about various other architects and builders.

Other individuals who shared knowledge and memories with me were Charles Belfoure, Adrienne Bell, George Benton, Randall Bierne, Louise Carlson, Randolph

Chalfant, Marcus Dagold, Rae DeDisse, James Dilts, Caroline Dixon, Elinor Ehle, Steven Fitch, Louise Flanigan, Paul Flynn, Patricia Fulton, Lottie Gerhardt, Dennis German, Dottie Grasty, Ruth Horn, Jacques Kelly, Barbara Lamb, Karen Lewand, Stephen McClain, Andrew O'Brien, Eugene O'Delle, E. Magruder Passano, Peter Pearre, F. Garner Ranney, Fred Rasmussen, Kathleen Rivelois, Sally Robinson, Walter Schamu, Eugene Servary, Edward Siekierski, Shreve Simpson, George Solter, Eileen Spring, Patrick Stambaugh, Jill Storms, Garth Thompson, Robert Vogelsang, James Waesche, James Wallon, Malcolm Warwick, Herbert Witz, and Barbara Young.

There are many whom I do not know by name. They, too, have my gratitude. Two groups come quickly to mind. First are the men and women who labor doing title searches in the land records offices of Baltimore City and Baltimore County. Recognizing my confusion when I ventured there, someone would invariably ask what I was looking for, then point the way and offer to carry the heavy volumes from shelf to work table and back.

In the second group are the receptionists and secretaries for the buildings and organizations I contacted. When I ex-

Greystone, University Parkway and 39th Street, n.d. (Private Collection.)

May, 2003. (Photo by David Prencipe.)

plained my purpose and what I wanted to know, the response was generally gracious and helpful, even though getting the information from their employers was difficult. I shall not forget the parking attendant who overheard my conversation, and then gave me the name and telephone number of a useful informant. When information was not forthcoming, I turned elsewhere. In only one instance did my inquiries fail completely.

Anyone who has had a book published is indebted to the people who know how to transform a manuscript into a bound volume—no easy task. My thanks first to the Maryland Historical Society for putting its time and energy into a local story. The people deserving my gratitude are the editors, Robert I. Cottom, Donna Blair Shear, and Patricia Dockman Anderson; various librarians, especially Francis O'Neill, and the photographer, overworked but always genial, David Prencipe.

Lastly, special thanks to John Higham whose keen editorial eye and historical sensibility increased my labors and thereby improved the manuscript.

Introduction

Tall oak, maple, locust, and ginkgo trees shading quiet streets. Small front gardens with ornamental trees and shrubs and a profusion of flowers from early spring to fall. Inviting Colonial and Tudor row homes, and alleys with fanciful decks and carefully tended gardens. A fringe of apartment buildings, some cold and imposing, others smaller and older, with a feeling of solid comfort and security. This is Tuscany-Canterbury, a North Baltimore neighborhood that is protected from the surrounding city by busy thoroughfares and one of the few remaining open streams in this part of the city. The Stony Run parallels Linkwood Road and provides the western boundary, with Warrenton Road on the north, University Parkway on the south, and Charles Street on the east. This small neighborhood, one of the most densely populated residential sections of Baltimore City, is home to 2,875 people.

What we know today as Tuscany-Canterbury developed slowly over a quarter of a century, beginning around the time of World War I, and remaining nameless until 1965. Before that it was part of the process of carving suburbs out of the countryside and the country estates around Baltimore City to create homes for the thriving upper and middle classes. This phenomenon was characteristic of most American cities in the years following the Civil War, along with population growth, business and industry, and transportation systems—and there is no apparent end in sight.

James Waesche gives a splendid account of early suburban development around Baltimore City in his history of Roland Park, *Crowning the Gravelly Hill.* The rapid growth of population and industry in nineteenth-century cities found municipal leaders ill-prepared to deal with the resulting problems. Increasingly dangerous living conditions and health concerns fostered a strong interest in a suburban or country life. Waesche vividly describes life in turn-of-the-century Baltimore:

Heat was only one of nineteenth-century Baltimore's disagreeable aspects, for the city was often choked by malodorous vapors that issued from thousands of privies (a 1900 estimate numbered them at 90,000). Public and private stables brewed their distinctive stenches, and open drains carried household wastes to streams and eventually the river, where it mixed with the stinking discharges— the fats, the offal, the chemicals—already dumped there by tanneries, canneries, slaughterhouses, fertilizer plants, and other components of the industrialized city. Many of those same factories spewed plumes of black coal smoke into the air—and although stylized plumes were engraved on letterheads as proud symbols of a company's productivity and prosperity, the real ones continuously precipitated noxious, gritty residue onto the city's streets and into the eyes and lungs of its residents.

The establishment of Roland Park and Guilford, to the north, west, and east of what would become Tuscany-Canterbury began around 1890 and continued into the second decade of the twentieth century. Why these two prestigious communities, Roland Park and Guilford, developed first and leapfrogged over and around an area that also adjoined the city, is conjectural. The Roland Park Company, ever on the alert for promising development opportunities, is silent on the subject. We might assume that the landholders of that part of the Clover Hill estate that eventually became Tuscany-Canterbury, would not sell to the Roland Park Company at an advantageous price. Or, alternatively, that this small, odd-shaped pocket of countryside did not lend itself to the grander designs of Edward Bouton, the director and supervisor of the Roland Park Company. Whatever the reasons for ignoring the Clover Hill farmland, later developers seized the opportunity to establish housing for a growing university population.

Tuscany-Canterbury

ONE

In the Beginning
From Gentry to Tradesmen

Turn back the calendar some three hundred years to the late seventeenth century. There one finds the beginning of the sequence of events that in time produced the Clover Hill estate and, much later, the Tuscany-Canterbury neighborhood. In 1688, Charles Merryman obtained 210 acres in a grant from Lord Baltimore who recorded it as "Merryman's Lott" in his rent book, "210 acres, yearly rent 8 shillings 5 pence. Merrymans Lott sur[veyed] 29 June 1688 for Charles Merryman on y N Side Jone's Falls." Descendants of Charles Merryman retained all or a part of this "Lott" for 181 years, until 1869, when Charles Reese of Baltimore, "dealer in wines, fruits and fine groceries" purchased it. The shift of land ownership from country gentleman to tradesman and entrepreneur was underway here and elsewhere.

The background of the initial land grant to Merryman deserves some explanation. Charles Calvert (1637–1715), Third Lord Baltimore, was a member of the English nobility. His grandfather, George Calvert (1580–1632), was an educated, politically astute, and ambitious man, who served on King James I's Privy Council and later as a close advisor to the king. The monarch rewarded his talents with a knighthood and with a large land grant in Ireland named the Manor of Baltimore. The little village of Baltimore exists to this day on the southwest tip of Ireland. When George Calvert converted to Catholicism around 1625, he resigned from government service, for, as a

Left: Clover Hill, 1869, nineteenth-century home of the Merryman family. The Guilford and Tuscany-Canterbury neighborhoods now occupy the 210-acre tract deeded to Charles Merryman in 1688. (Episcopal Archives.)

Charles Calvert (1637–1715), Third Lord Baltimore, awarded tracts such as "Merryman's Lott" as incentives to encourage settlement in the Chesapeake colony. (Maryland Historical Society.)

Catholic, he could no longer recognize a Protestant king as the ultimate authority. In consideration of George's years of loyal service, King James awarded him the title, Baron of Baltimore.

The Calvert Family

Drawn by visions of wealth in the New World, George had already invested in various colonizing companies, but he also wanted a colony of his own—both as a financial investment and as a haven for English Catholics. Accordingly, he obtained a grant from the king for land in Newfoundland. There he hoped to attract English settlers and to engage in farming and fishing. The quaint and inaccurate notions about geography and climate did not prepare him for the hardships he would encounter at that latitude. The Avalon settlement failed and the Calvert party returned home late in 1629. (The Elizabethans did not know that the Gulf

Stream, which warmed their island, veered away from Newfoundland, leaving that land to the mercies of the Labrador Sea.) Still determined to establish a New World colony, he applied again to the king, now Charles I, successor to James, for another grant, this time north of Virginia, along the Chesapeake.

Unfortunately, George did not live to see this beautiful and bounteous colony, named Maryland, in honor of Charles I's wife, Queen Henrietta Maria. The grant passed to Calvert's eldest son, Cecil, who became the first Proprietor of Maryland and the second Lord Baltimore upon his father's death in 1632.

Cecil never visited his colony in the New World. He could best protect his interests by remaining close to court. The Maryland colony stood in an especially precarious position as a Catholic settlement. Rather than lead the expedition himself, Cecil appointed his brother Leonard as first governor of Maryland. In the aristocratic tradition of primogeniture inheritance, Charles followed his father as proprietor in 1675—and it is in his lordship's rent books that the Merryman's Lott entry is found.

In regard to land distribution, Lord Baltimore's "Conditions of Plantation" contained specific instructions to the colonists for allotment. The four steps to land ownership involved the petition, the warrant, the survey, and the patent processes. The settler, in this case Merryman, petitioned the governor for a specific piece of land. The governor then approved the petition and issued a warrant to lay out the tract. Surveyors measured off the claim and drew the plat, a detailed drawing of the property lines. In the final step, the patent, the property owner gained secure title to his land. In their feudal-like role as proprietors of the Maryland colony, successive Lords

Baltimore collected a token "quit rent" from landholders. Hence, Charles Merryman received title to his lot and paid a yearly rent. This small piece of land became a farm named Clover Hill. The story is a fundamental piece of Merryman family history.

The Merryman Family

The name Merryman first appeared in the New World early in the seventeenth century. Some time "before 1650" Charles Merryman lived in Lancaster County, Virginia, where he worked as a wheelwright. This must have been a profitable business, for he moved to Maryland and purchased land. Additional tracts granted in 1694, 1703, and l704, carried fanciful and informative names such as Merryman's Addition, Merryman's Beginning, and Merryman's Pasture. Together with Merryman's Lott and these successive purchases, Charles owned more than a thousand acres between the Patapsco and Back Rivers. He became a planter and a captain in the militia—a person of consequence in the region. Perhaps as a reward for his loyal service, Lord Baltimore gave him these various tracts of land.

There is no record that Charles Merryman ever lived on Merryman's Lott. The first to do so was his second son, John, who in 1714 received half of Merryman's Lott, and some other acreage "for the fatherly love and affection that I Bear unto my Sec'd son John Merryman for Divers good Causes and other Considerations." After his father's death in 1725, John Merryman cleared the land and established a farm and a home that he then named Clover Hill. For the next 155 years the Merryman family occupied and operated the farm at Clover Hill, selling it in 1869. The name Clover Hill remains with

us to this day, albeit spelled Cloverhill—one of the principal streets of Tuscany-Canterbury.

The Merryman name was used early in the nineteenth century to designate an important road, Merryman's Lane. A century or so later, in 1929, it was renamed University Parkway by the Johns Hopkins University, the more powerful neighbor immediately to the south of the Clover Hill farm. Merryman's Court, located in the Keswick section of Roland Park, is the only surviving reminder of the family who once owned all the land from the Jones Falls to York Road, and from University Parkway some distance to the north. While the farm and the family name receded into history, the family itself survived and prospered. They moved farther north and established another productive farm, Hayfields near Hunt Valley. Merryman family histories suggest that the "Hayfield Merrymans" might not be migrants from the Clover Hill Farm. After almost 125 years, the Merrymans sold that farm, too, this time not to a tradesman but to a developer. Hayfields is now a golf course and country club. Such are the changes in land use between the early eighteenth and late twentieth centuries. Of the many Merrymans living today, John owns a farm in Parkton that he calls Cloverhill, in memory of the original:

Cloverhill Farm has been in my family since the early 1700s. The first John was a merchant; if you were successful, you bought land and moved out to the country. John was the first Merryman to go to Hereford. He was a large landowner and he is buried in Hereford. John of Calvert Street was the first Mayor of Baltimore; he was active in the Revolutionary War. George Merryman owned the land which became Johns Hopkins University. Nicholas Merryman Bosley bought and built up

Tuscany-Canterbury

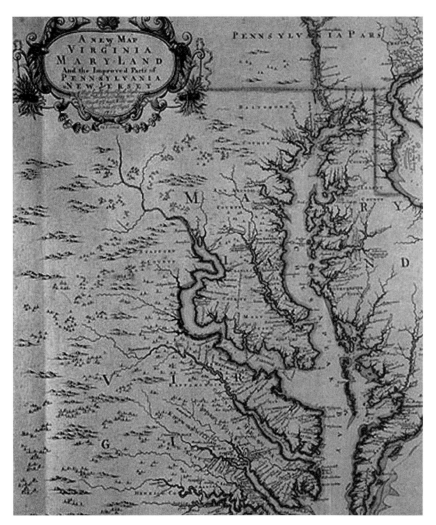

John Senex, A New Map of Virginia and Maryland and Improved Parts of Pennsylvania and New Jersey, 1721. *Merryman settled in Baltimore County, just north of the Patapsco River, shown here in the top center. (Maryland Historical Society.)*

Bryn Mawr School may have been left by hunting parties roaming the forest, or, as some suggest, from the Archaic period of between three and four thousand years ago.

The land owned by Charles Merryman, and later John Merryman, lay along the valley of a small stream, eventually called the Stony Run. Up until about 1650 the valley remained a wilderness. An evocative twentieth-century account is William Marye's description of the valley of the Stony Run as ". . . desolate, mournful, mysterious, hostile and forbidding. Wild beasts, now long extinct in these parts, roamed the valley unmolested by man — bears, wolves, and panther. So, too, the beaver." Surely deer, small game, fish, and birds also inhabited the primeval forest. There is no record of how the land granted to John Merryman in 1714 was used prior to that time. Marye's description of the valley is as much as we now know. Historians tell us that land "use" began when European settlers occupied and tilled the forest for agricultural purposes.

Apparently, John Merryman was the first person to clear the land along the valley of the Stony Run. He built a house, located where the residence of the Bishop of the Cathedral of the Incarnation stands today, and established a farm, encompassing perhaps several hundred acres—Clover Hill. The farm occupied the land on either side of what is now Charles Street. As was customary at the time, he located his house on a hill, or on elevated ground, close to a spring or other source of water. The very early settlers did not dig wells.

If John had difficulty developing a farm, he left no record of it, but there is reason to believe that the enterprise was not easy. Geologically, this area is on the coastal plain of the Piedmont, created as the land descends from the Appalachians to the sea,

Hayfields. I am the oldest son of an oldest son of an oldest son. Cloverhill Farm here in Parkton grows clover very well.

Before Clover Hill

What of the land itself? What did it look like to those first colonists arriving on these shores early in the seventeenth century? This was part of a vast wilderness, described as "a perfect forest" in an early chronicle of the eastern seaboard. Oak and chestnut were the principal trees of the forest all along the Chesapeake. Insofar as we know, not even Indians disturbed the forces of nature in this small corner of the colony. The few remnants of Indian habitation discovered at the site of the

with soil composed mainly of silt, clay, and gravel, certainly not the best for farming. Moreover, Merryman's Lott was located on a gravely ridge, subsequently known as Little Britain Ridge, that extended from the Jones Falls to Herring Run. William Marye's history of the Stony Run Valley states that much of the land remained "vacant and without owners" because it was not good for farming. Situated mainly on wooded

Map of Stony Run Valley. Note the lost landmarks placed among the the present-day streets and buildings. (Maryland Historical Magazine.)

STONY RUN VALLEY

7

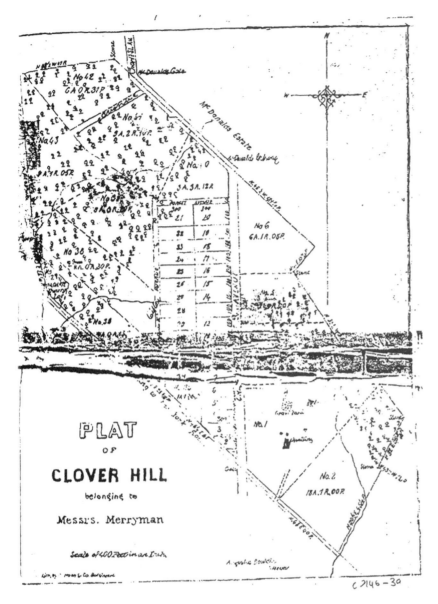

Charles Merryman's descendents divided and sold the farm in 1865 and 1869. (Maryland State Archives.)

where manpower was the only power. His will, dated 1749, indicated that he owned cattle, sheep, and horses, the latter probably used for transportation, as the horse collar and the plow did not become widely available until the late eighteenth and early nineteenth century. Some 120 years later, one family member described the first Clover Hill as "a typical farm . . . with wheat, corn, and oats being grown, cattle, hogs, chickens, and turkeys raised, and an apple orchard flourishing."

There are few substantiating records, but the Merryman family certainly erected an assortment of buildings to house the family and its slaves, and the farm undoubtedly required numerous outbuildings as well. At some point in the late eighteenth or early nineteenth century, the family built a grand homestead on the farmland situated east of Charles Street. It eventually became part of Guilford. The Episcopal Diocese purchased the homestead in 1910 and it now serves as the bishop's home. It is visible today from Bishops Road, a solid, square, three-story stone residence with a mansard roof, set well back on spacious grounds. Although no surviving records indicate that Clover Hill was a financially successful enterprise, the size and quality of the homestead suggests wealth. Or, did the wealth stem from selling parts of the farm to successful Baltimore businessmen?

In the Land Records Office of Baltimore City, a deed dated October 29, 1865 states that the will of Charles Merryman transferred the Clover Hill property to eight of his descendants. The heirs then sold the Clover Hill farm in 1869 to Charles Reese, who named it Enderby. Reese transformed Clover Hill from a farm operated by landed gentry to a country estate, the home of a successful tradesman. The shift in function, from farm to estate, is mirrored by the change in name, from Clover Hill to the

slopes, instead of open bottomlands, farms here required more labor-intensive clearing as a first step to agriculture. How much of the land was cleared at the time of John's death about thirty-five years later is not known. What is known is that English settlers cleared the land, possibly by burning trees, then digging out the stumps. They used hoes, axes, and eventually plows for cultivation. Since John is said to have "owned scores of slaves," it is reasonable to suppose that Clover Hill was a working farm rather than open country. Certainly he needed many laborers to operate a farm

more pretentious Enderby. Reese gentrified the Merryman homestead extensively (rooflines, extensions, porches, landscaping), but what he did with the farm is not recorded.

Much of the farm lying west of Charles Street apparently remained within the Merryman family, and the specific changes in ownership are well recorded in the Baltimore County Land Records office. Court clerks recorded forty-one transactions between various Merrymans and others between 1858 and 1874, many clearly pertaining to this area.

Of the various subsequent sales, the one that interests us most occurred on April 12, 1878. On that date the "parcel of land lying on the East side of Charles Street Avenue . . . being part of the Clover Hill estate," was sold to Arunah S. Abell. The eight-acre parcel sold for nine thousand dollars, with the conditions that "no glue factory, slaughter house, tavern or brewery or place where liquor is to be sold or

This historic marker stands on Charles Street just north of University Parkway on the Guilford side of the street. (Photo by David Prencipe.)

manufactured, blacksmith shop or any other manufactory or anything that can be considered a nuisance shall be erected upon the above described land."

Maps of Baltimore City and County from 1850 onward enhance the story begun in the land records. First and foremost among these maps is the delightfully detailed G. M. Hopkins 1876 *Atlas of Baltimore, Maryland and Environs.* Hopkins, a surveyor and book publisher, was employed by the Library of

Clover Hill, c. 1869. (Episcopal Archives.)

Tuscany-Canterbury

*Clover Hill, shown on
G. M. Hopkins' 1876
Atlas of Baltimore,
Maryland and Environs.
(Philadelphia:
F. Bourquin, 1876.)*

Congress. He included property and people in his maps in addition to roads and topography, providing later viewers with a glimpse of the social history of the time. Anyone may look at this wonderful map, shown above, in the Special Collections reading room of the Maryland Historical Society.

What do we see? First the roads, Charles Street Avenue and Merryman's Lane with a tollgate at the intersection, Melrose Avenue now Canterbury Road and Forest Street, subsequently Mallory Lane and now Highfield Road. Sixth Avenue is now 39th Street. Most surprisingly, the area now occupied by Canterbury and Cloverhill was laid out into the thirty-five or thirty-six lots we see today. The land was divided into eleven parcels, seven owned by various Merrymans. The Colonnade now occupies the tract labeled the A. Gaddes Estate.

Eighteen structures are depicted, six of them clearly houses, the rest various outbuildings. Along the Stony Run was a millrace extending from a large mill pond situated just south of Cold Spring Lane that provided power for the Paradise Mill, located somewhere between Ridgemede and Stoneyford Roads. A narrow gauge railroad ran along the Stony Run. Closer to Merryman's Lane was a quarry, the site clearly visible on the map from Linkwood Road.

Thomas M. Ward's 1894 *The City of Baltimore Topographical Survey* (available from the Maps and Records section of the Baltimore City Department of Public Works) showed few changes. Melrose Avenue had become Ash Avenue. There were six small farms and about twenty houses and outbuildings. The half-dozen

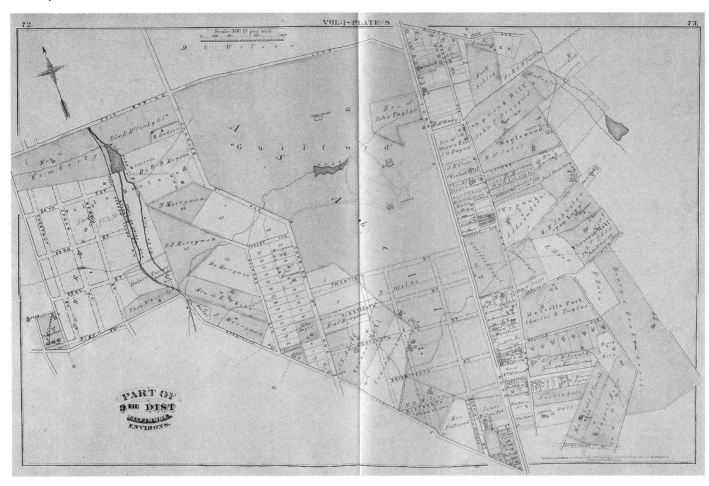

Clover Hill, c. 1869.

large structures along Charles Street Avenue between Merryman's Lane and Forest Avenue (now Highfield Road) show the great mansions that the Solter, Hyde, and Duker families built along the toll road. Residents cultivated about half the land and the rest remained forest. This was truly rural countryside. The transition from rural to suburban was well underway elsewhere around the city, fostered by the growth of streets, railroads, and other forms of public transportation. It was not until the 1890s, however, that suburbanization began in our own backyard. Roland Park was being built, and Guilford was waiting in the wings. Tuscany-Canterbury's turn came twenty-five years later.

TWO

The Boundaries
of Tuscany-Canterbury

We can see the neighborhood's beginning in the 1912 Maryland Geological Survey and in the Topographical Survey Commission's 1914 *Atlas of Baltimore City.* Tuscany-Canterbury stood on the eve of suburbanization. The major roads are there, albeit often with strange names. Real estate companies such as the University Parkway Company replaced estates. Not a trace of their plans for University Heights and University Circle remains today. We now have Tuscany and Ridgemede. The many great old houses with their owners' names are clearly depicted on those early twentieth-century maps. Their disappearance is part of the story of Charles Street's development, recounted in the next chapter. The one building we all recognize,

now eighty-nine years old, is Canterbury Hall.

Charles Street, University Parkway, Linkwood Road, and Warrenton Road are the boundaries of Tuscany-Canterbury, and each has a history relevant to the neighborhood. Three of them are arbitrary and man-made. The fourth, Linkwood, is defined by the Stony Run, a portion of Clover Hill farm's original western boundary. The farm sprawled considerably beyond the current boundaries until the needs and predilections of man and his institutions imposed limits. The growth of roads from the city to the country, and the activities established along these roads, affected the ways in which this community developed.

Charles Street, c. 1931. (Maryland Historical Society.)

The original entrance to Homewood, 1933. (Maryland Historical Society.)

Charles Street, for example, bisected the Clover Hill farm. The portion to the east, with its solid and attractive stone Merryman homestead, gradually became Arunah S. Abell's Guilford estate. The *Baltimore Sun* owner purchased the farm from land speculator William McDonald who named it after the battle of Guilford Courthouse (North Carolina) where he was wounded during the American Revolution. William's son built the extravagant Italianate house that the Abell family used as a summer

Charles Street, shown here on the left as Forrest Street, is one of Baltimore's oldest roads. (Baltimore in 1752. From a Sketch then made by John Moale Esqr. deceased, corrected by the late Daniel Bowley Esqr.)

home until 1907 when Arunah's heirs sold it to the Guilford Company. The outline of this gracious new residential area took shape in the early years of the last century as grand houses set on spacious lawns emerged from farmland and woods. The western portion become Tuscany-Canterbury with houses fronting and serving the toll road, and farm buildings farther back bespoke more utilitarian usage.

Charles Street

Charles Street had modest beginnings. Lore has it that it follows a Susquehannock Indian trail. In October 1935, "a real Indian, a painted Indian, astride a horse" led a parade celebrating the twentieth anniversary of the Charles Street Association. A less romantic view is that Charles Street followed an old wagon path. Known first as Forrest Street when "Baltimore Town" was laid out in 1730, it led north from the harbor "toward and through woodlands and farms" to the great forest that still surrounded the fledgling city.

Sometime in the ensuing three or four decades, Forrest Street became Charles Street, perhaps in honor of Charles Calvert, fifth Lord Baltimore or Charles Carroll the Barrister, a Baltimore Iron Works investor. The street grew with the city, extending north of Merryman's Lane by 1854 and paved with cobblestones, wooden blocks, granite blocks, and asphalt blocks, until the 1920s, when smooth asphalt paving covered the road. Trolley tracks were installed in 1871 in the downtown section. After they were removed in 1940 and the street re-paved, the *Baltimore Sun* reported, "The street is smooth as a billiard table and a free place to park."

As early as 1804, Baltimore constructed toll roads that connected the interior of the country to the harbor and promoted transportation and economic growth. In 1858 a toll-gate was installed at the corner of Charles Street and Merryman's Lane, despite protest by the residents on the avenue. David Perine, the owner of "Homeland," objected to chartering the turnpike and so did Samuel Wyman, who had just purchased "Homewood" from the Carroll family. William Hollifield reported in his *History of the Turnpikes of Baltimore City and County* that Wyman anticipated his new purchase as the place "where he would be enabled to spend in comparative seclusion the remainder of his days and where he could indulge without unpleasant intrusions, his horticultural and rural tastes." "The road," he said, "would destroy his privacy and seclusion, and his vines, fruit trees, garden, and orchard would be utterly destroyed or made valueless by being exposed to constant depredations from rowdies and others attracted from the neighboring city." This impassioned protest failed and the four and one-half-mile toll road from 24th Street to Powder Mill Road

(now Bellona Avenue) opened to the delight of many. An anonymous admirer wrote:

The road is lined for much of its length with large trees, whose overhanging branches entwine in the center, cutting off the sharp

Guilford, the Abell family summer home. (Maryland Historical Society.)

Miss Belle O'Brien, c. 1910. Property owners objected to the tollhouse, installed in 1858 at the corner of Charles Street and Merryman's Lane. (Bryden Hyde.)

*Ray Hyde at Belle Lawn,
c. 1910. (Bryden Hyde.)*

*Belle Lawn, c. 1910,
home of the Hyde family.
(Bryden Hyde.)*

rays of the sun and presenting a vista of rare beauty. The road itself is rolling, but with no steep ascents. Branching off from it throughout its entire length are avenues and private roads which lead to country homes. The Avenue is one of the most popular pleasure drives out of Baltimore. This is so by reason of the varied beauty of the adjacent country and because many prominent citizens of the city have purchased adjoining ground and built magnificent residences for summer homes.

Jeremiah D. Mallory purchased land from Martha Merryman in 1881 and built one of these "magnificent residences," located on Charles Street Avenue and Mallory Lane (now Highfield Road). Mallory was a well-known businessman whose company

manufactured equipment for trains. George A. Frederick designed this "elegant and capacious dwelling." The description in the *Maryland Journal* of September, 1883, is positively rhapsodic:

The style is Queen Anne's, and the steep roofs, the many gables and deeply recessed and canopied windows, spacious porches and ornamental timber work make a varied and pleasing appearance. The halls and vestibules are finished throughout in polished ash, as are all the rooms of the first and second floors [and all] are laid with the encaustic tile. . . . The windows have all mullioned transoms, filled with the richest stained and jeweled glass, with French plate in the lower lights . . . [and the stable] 30 feet wide and 60 feet long, two stories

Major Hyde's Crown Lunch Room, c. 1900. (Bryden Hyde.)

Major George Washington Hyde, c. 1915. (Bryden Hyde.)

high, covered with slate, surmounted with a picturesque turret.

At least a half-dozen other great mansions were built along Charles Street Avenue between Mallory Lane and Merryman's Lane. Major George Washington Hyde, landowner and businessman, built a twenty-three-room house, replete with turret, gables, and porches in 1880. He named his domain Belle Lawn. C. Preston Scheffanacker's affectionate recollections of his boyhood visits to this extravagant structure around 1910 described a large family with four servants, a cook, a handyman, and a laundress. He recalled a vegetable garden for the family with enough "to put up" for the winter, and chickens, cows, and two horses, the latter used to drive the major around to oversee his business enterprises. The most notable was the Crown Lunch Room at 225 East Baltimore Street that operated on the "honor system" until World War II. One of the major's properties was the Canterbury and Cloverhill acreage, later sold to University Homes, of which George W. Morris, the developer, was president.

One of the major's sons, sixty-three year-old-Ray Hyde, wrote a charming memoir,

published in *The Sun*, November 13, 1949, about that moment in the history of Tuscany-Canterbury:

My family lived in a big house on rocky Charles Street Avenue right across from the Abell grounds . . . some of my city friends hesitated to visit us at night: they didn't like traveling the lonely roads. . . . Looking back, I suppose we were pretty far out. But my friends and I always had plenty of fun fooling around Abell's lake [now Sherwood Gardens] and exploring the Abell estate. . . . I rode my bicycle a lot . . . with Ed and Phil Schmidt, who lived just north of the toll house on Charles and Merryman's Lane . . . when I had no money to pay the toll, I could leave the road, take my bike through the Schmidts' yard and around the back of the toll house and come out on the other side of the gate. I can still see Miss Belle O'Brien, who collected the tolls, waving a finger at the Schmidts and me and saying, "You boys shouldn't do that. It isn't honest." It cost three cents to take a bicycle past the tollgate, and to a boy in 1898 that was a lot of money.

The neighborhood began losing its country atmosphere around 1906,when my father

Phillipshurst, c. 1900, home of George T. Phillips. (William Hollifield.)

Everbright, c. 1900, home of the Dulaneys, stood on the corner of Charles Street and Mallory Lane, now Highfield Road. (Private Collection.)

began selling his land just above the tollgate for building lots. But the big change didn't come until 1912, the year the Roland Park Company began the Guilford development. I remember the year because I got married during it.

George T. Phillips, president of a Baltimore cannery, spent $40,000 (approximately half a million dollars today) and built another of these extravagant houses, Phillipshurst, south of the present Scottish Rite Temple. A postcard depicting the house with a note on the reverse reads, "Dear Tom. This shows the garage connected to the house by a bridge. The boy has an automobile of his own. There is a bathroom for every two bedrooms — and there are 15 bedrooms — and so many balconies."

Other large homes, somewhat less extravagant, belonged to the Carters, the Dukers, and the Dulaneys. The last, Everbright, was a warm and welcoming home on the corner of Charles Street Avenue and Mallory Lane (now Highfield Road). One of them, located on the site of the Scottish Rite Temple, was moved cater-corner across the street and remains there to this day at 3901 North Charles Street. The Baltimore City topographical map of 1914 shows all of these houses, with the owners' names.

Between the two world wars and afterward, the big houses on Charles Street

Grand homes rose on the former Merryman land at the turn of the last century. (The 1914 Atlas of the City of Baltimore, Maryland, made from surveys and official Plans by the Topographical Survey Commission, Joseph W. Shirley, Chief Engineer [Baltimore, 1914].)

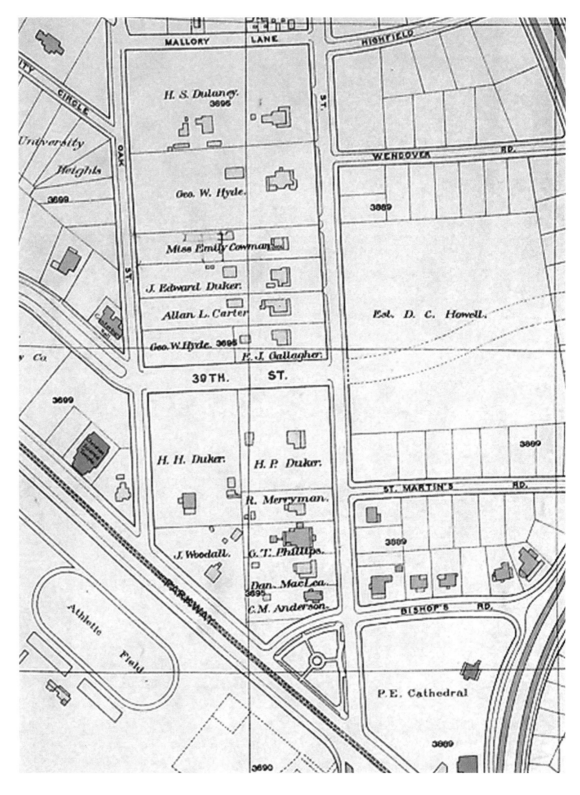

Avenue disappeared. This is surprising as their owners obviously took great pride in them and in the symbolism of being able to live in a suburban area, close to the countryside estates and the prestigious communities of North Baltimore. All were solid men of business, involved in various manufacturing enterprises. What happened is a cautionary tale.

These grandiose designs may have contributed to their demise. Many had large rooms with high ceilings and inadequate insulation to withstand the cold winters and in the critical depression years of the 1930s, the cost of heating the large houses with coal became exorbitant. Families who wished to sell were unable to find a buyer.

Two years before the 1929 stock market crash, however, the large lot at 3908 did sell. On it rose the Warrington, an enormous and expensive apartment house begun in the last months of prosperity and optimism. A former resident recalled the neighborhood in turmoil about zoning changes that would permit a building higher than two or three stories. A somewhat similar problem occurred with the Northway several years later. The Cathedral of the Incarnation opposed a high-rise on the opposite side of the street, eventually forcing a design change to its present step-back, ziggurat facade. At the time residents strenuously objected to turning Charles Street into a veritable "Chinese wall" of apartment houses.

As the Depression wore on, the solution for many of the other houses was to cut them up into rental apartments. The pre-sence of one such "residence turned apartment house"—and of a true apartment house—opened the door to further development. When several smaller house lots became available, Mullan built the Cambridge at 3900 North Charles Street. Phillipshurst burned in the 1920s to be replaced by the Buckingham Arms, which also burned in 1983, then by the St. James, built in 1989, which is likely to endure for the ages. Everbright lasted somewhat longer before making way for Highfield House. The fate of Mallory's magnificent mansion in the early part of the century is unclear. A resident of that period described a haunted house that may have been Mallory's. In our time, the site was a vacant, weed-grown lot that has become the Winthrop House condominiums.

The Hyde family at Belle Lawn, c. 1910. (Bryden Hyde.)

The Warrington Apartments, 1928, first of the neighborhood's high rise structures. (Maryland Historical Society.)

Belle Lawn, n.d (Bryden Hyde.)

A truly grande dame, now on the verge of her tenth decade, who was born and grew up in one of these Charles Street Avenue mansions, makes that time come alive again:

I lived at 3904 Charles Street when Charles Street was a dirt road north of University Parkway, and there was a tollbooth right where the Confederate statue is now. I was born in that house and I lived there until the 1940s. *There were big houses all along the street — ours, the Hydes', the Carters', the Dulaneys', and on the other side of Mallory Lane [now Highfield Road] an enormous Victorian house that we called the haunted house, because it was empty, with weeds all over the yard. All these houses had artesian wells and cisterns because the city water wasn't out here yet. My parents moved here because it was "the place" to live then.*

Our house was built from lumber that had been used in the Philadelphia Centennial of 1875. When those buildings were taken down, the lumber was floated down to Baltimore on a barge and used for buildings here. Our house was very cold because there was nothing between the clapboards and the plaster. The living room had fourteen-foot ceilings and a huge fireplace. There was a center hall, so the air would blow through the house in the summer. There were shutters on the inside to close when the sun came in.

All the houses had big yards and the back yard went all the way to Canterbury Road. We had a croquet set in the front yard and neighbors came to play with us. We also

Charles Street Avenue, c. 1900. (Private Collection.)

22

played a wonderful game, Kick the Can, for hours on end. There were stables in the back yard because everybody had a horse and carriage. One house up the street had a cow tethered in the yard. My nurse would walk up there with me to see the cow. We also had a huge cherry tree, full of black cherries like we buy in the market now. We children would climb up that tree and eat and eat. I remember the lamplighter. He would come along, climb a little ladder and light each lamp. I was terrified of him because he talked and hollered to himself all the time.

In 1917 my mother bought a Dodge automobile and we got rid of the horse and carriage. My father drove us to school in that car. My brother went to Boys' Latin, I went to Bryn Mawr and my sister went to Calvert. They were all downtown then. My mother was a Goucher graduate, which was unusual because not many women went to college then. My mother spent all her time climbing the genealogy tree. I went to Smith because after twelve years at Bryn Mawr, I didn't want to go to Bryn Mawr (the College) again.

Mallory Lane had a row of dumpy little houses behind the haunted house. A family with lots of children lived in one of them. The father had died so they didn't have much money. The children wandered around the neighborhood with torn clothing and dirty faces; we stayed away from them.

I remember when George Morris came around to all of the neighbors with his plan to build row houses in the back of our houses. He persuaded everybody to sell the back of their lots so that he could develop them. He said we would have a nice alley at the back of our yards, but there was a twenty-foot drop instead, and my father had to put up a retaining wall. The alley had garages that went under the houses on Cloverhill, but they couldn't use the garages in the winter because the cars couldn't get through the snow.

The backyard at Everbright, c. 1900. (Private Collection.)

The Confederate Women's monument, erected in 1918, stands on the spot where the tollgate operated until 1906. (Maryland Historical Society.)

Another major change on Charles Street Avenue was the loss of the tollgate and house. Erected in 1858 on the corner of Charles Street and University Parkway (then Merryman's Lane), it operated until 1906. The last tollkeeper, Belle O'Brien, was, apparently, a much-loved neighborhood fixture. In 1918, the Maryland Daughters of the Confederacy, with donations from the state and various private individuals, erected

The tollgate is shown on this map, bottom right. (G. M. Hopkins, 1876 Atlas of Baltimore, Maryland and Environs.)

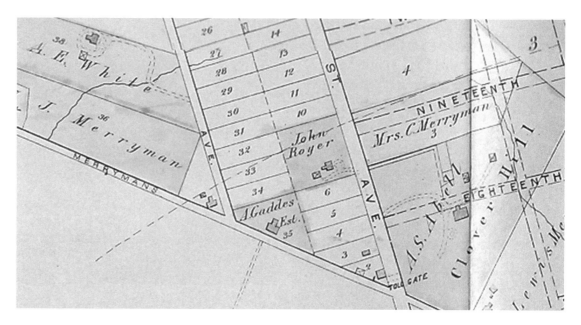

Merryman's Lane became University Parkway in 1914. (Topographical Survey, 1914.)

wounded and exhausted solder who still holds his furled and fallen flag. An epitaph chiseled on the plinth commemorates the courage of Confederate women: "In Difficulty and Danger/Regardless of Self; They Fed the Hungry/Clothed the Needy/ Nursed the Wounded/and/Comforted the Dying." The sculptor was J. Maxwell Miller who used Baltimore County policeman Martin L. Chenoweth as the model for the wounded soldier. An admirer described the officer's physique as "the best . . . ever seen."

From Indian path or wagon path, Charles Street grew to ten and a half miles, from the harbor markets, past the edifices of commerce, the grand houses, cultural, educational, and religious institutions, to the leafy suburbs, and to Baltimore County.

University Parkway

University Parkway began as Merryman's Lane and connected the York Road to the Jones Falls. The impetus for the lane came about in the first few years of the nineteenth century when John Merryman sold some of his land to Charles Carroll of Carrollton. Carroll then built Homewood

a statue at this intersection dedicated "To the Confederate Women of Maryland, 1861–1865." High on a red granite plinth, the bronze statue memorializes "The Brave at Home." Two women, one in a billowing dress and cape, stand proudly erect, displaying strength and fortitude in time of adversity. One supports and comforts a

as a wedding gift for his son. Merryman's Lane became the entrance to the new household that is now the "architectural jewel" of the Johns Hopkins University campus.

In the 1890s, when Edward Bouton was planning Roland Park, the lane was still a lane, alternately dusty and muddy. It crossed the Stony Run over a narrow iron bridge and passed a tavern that stood on the site of the present-day Tudor Arms Apartments. The transformation of Merryman's Lane to a broad thoroughfare came about because Bouton had decidedly upscale intentions for his real estate venture.

The problem of devising a "grand approach" to Roland Park vexed Bouton for some time. His letter to the Olmsted firm, the landscape architects for Roland Park,

(Bryden Hyde.)

outlined a solution. "It has occurred to me that Charles Street Avenue might be utilized as far as Merryman's Lane and Merryman's Lane widened from Charles Street Avenue to Cedar Avenue, or to whatever point our proposed driveway would

Abell's lake, c. 1890.
(Bryden Hyde.)

*"Heavy traffic on
Charles Street," c. 1900.
(Bryden Hyde.)*

name changed to University Parkway in
1914. The Olmsted firm designed the
parkway, filling in the intersections and
dividing it into an upper and lower section,
as it wound uphill toward Roland Avenue.

Linkwood and Stony Run

The history of Linkwood Road is, in fact,
the history of Stony Run, which it parallels.
It is difficult to believe, as we look at the
gently gurgling stream we see today, that
the Stony Run once supported "no less than
four grist mills, three of which were in
operation at the same time." At least one of
the four, Paradise Mill, was located within
the boundaries of Tuscany- Canterbury on
land once owned by the Merrymans.
Compared to the Jones Falls, the Gunpow-
der, the Gywnns Falls, or to Herring Run,
the Stony Run was classified as a "weak
stream," with a horsepower of merely
twenty when compared to two hundred
fifty for the Jones Falls.

leave Merryman's Lane on its way to
Roland Avenue." Bouton planned to "see
the owners of the Charles Street Avenue
turnpike . . . to arrange that no tolls should
be collected from pleasure vehicles which
turn into Merryman's Lane." He also hoped
that "the Johns Hopkins would be willing
to cooperate in widening and improving
Merryman's Lane past their property."

And so it came to pass. The lane was
widened and improved in 1903 and the

Stony Run, earlier known as Union Run,
rises in a lake on the Elkridge Country

*Hyde family. (Bryden
Hyde.)*

26

Club grounds. It has little strength or power until it joins several tributaries. The first is located just above Cold Spring Lane and the others along Linkwood. The Homeland branch rises in the vicinity of Northern Parkway and Bellona Avenue, meanders through Homeland and its lakes, past Notre Dame, Evergreen, and Loyola, and passes under Charles Street before it joins Stony Run.

The Guilford branch, or so I will call it, begins in the vicinity of Sherwood Gardens, where there was once a shallow boating lake, created when the young William McDonald diverted and dammed several streams. Confined in a tunnel under Charles Street, it emerges briefly behind the houses on West Highfield, only to be channeled again into a tunnel under the grounds of Calvert School, emerging as it enters the Stony Run near Stoneyford Road. The open segment of this otherwise invisible brook is a delight to see, twisting and bubbling happily over rocks and through a heavily wooded gully. Go there, shut out the noise of the traffic on Charles Street, turn your back to Oak Place, and you will sense what was here long ago. Many other springs and tiny brooks, no longer visible, fed the waterway that once powered several gristmills.

Paradise Mill, also known as Van Bibber's Mill, stood on what is now Linkwood Road a few yards north of the intersection with Stoneyford Road. An 1850 map of the city and the county shows the mill and a few adjacent structures. An 1876 map shows the mill, and the millrace rising from a sizable mill pond just south of Cold Spring Lane, then swinging to the east of the Stony Run to power the mill. A tax list of the "Patapsco Lower Hundred 1799–1800" describes the site of the mill, "190 acres say 188 — a Thundergrist Mill — a 2 sto[ry] mill house of stone very rough and com[mon] 32 by 18. The stream on which the mill is fixed is quite insufficient to work her." The mill changed hands many times, once for three thousand dollars, but there is

no record of its abandonment. All that remains of that era is a millstone marking the entrance to the Linkwood Apartments located on the western bank of the Stony Run.

While the era of the mills lies beyond the memory of people living here today, many recall the Ma and Pa Railroad that traveled up the valley of the Stony Run. It began as a narrow-gauge railway in 1882 (anticipated in the narrow gauge track appearing in the earlier G. M. Hopkins map of 1876). The tracks were converted to standard gauge in 1901 and formally named the Maryland and Pennsylvania Railroad. Before that year, the narrow gauge system was known variously as the Baltimore and Delta, the Maryland Central, and the

The Maryland and Pennsylvania Railroad, 1954. The train wound through the Stony Run Valley until 1958. (James P. Gallagher in Rudy Fischer Collection.)

Baltimore and Lehigh. Officially the Maryland and Pennsylvania Railroad began at North Avenue and Howard Street and terminated in York, Pennsylvania, conveying passengers, coal, and farm products along its route. The little engines that could, and did, struggled with steep grades and sharp curves for more than fifty years before their runs ended in 1958. The railroad enlivened this otherwise quiet neighborhood, marking the time of day and exciting the children. Those who remember the Ma and Pa miss it still. One proper and learned person of my acquaintance fondly recalls waving at the engineer as she walked to work. She is not alone in her affection for this railroad. The Maryland and Pennsylvania Railroad Preservation and Historical Society has regular meetings and an active membership. Its roadbed in Baltimore County is a popular destination for hikers and cyclists on pleasant weekend afternoons.

Today children and dog-walkers enjoy the park along the valley of the Stony Run that is but a small remnant of the "chain of parks" envisioned by the Olmsted Brothers and planned by the city parks department. Beginning with Druid Hill Park and traversing Wyman Park through the valleys of the Jones Falls and of the Stony Run and thence to Lake Roland, a vast public space that graces the urban landscape might have been and could still be achieved. This could only be possible if the owners of the great estates along the way could be persuaded to release some acreage, as did Samuel Wyman. A long report in the *Baltimore Sun*,

October 16, 1905, predicted that "the whole Stony Run valley will be turned into a place of beauty and pleasure."

Linkwood Road was opened in 1917. The name is English in origin. Linkwood was the name that Hugh Hampton Young, a prominent physician and owner of a considerable estate in the area, gave to his holdings. His home was located at the intersection of Linkwood Road and Cold Spring Lane, the site of Loyola College resident student housing, Wynnewood Towers.

Warrenton Road

Warrenton Road is the southern boundary of Guilford on the west side of Charles Street. This rather odd-shaped wedge of land detached from the main body of Guilford is a conundrum. Why is it part of Guilford rather than of Tuscany-Canterbury? Roland Park/Guilford promoter Edward Bouton wanted to connect his two prestigious suburbs, and the streets from Warrenton to Cold Spring Lane became the bridge. Houses on both sides of Warrenton Road belong to Guilford and Tuscany-Canterbury begins in Warrenton's backyards. One of these backyards holds a beautiful stand of woods with fox, owls, and other wildlife. Great waves of daffodils cover it in the spring and the property extends all the way to Tuscany Road. Quite recently a family of yellow-crowned night herons has taken up residence in the woods and has begun fishing in the Stony Run.

THREE

Building a Neighborhood

Described by a long-time resident in the May 22, 1994 issue of the *Sun* as "this quiet little valley in among mountains of high rises," Tuscany-Canterbury as we know it today was built mainly between the two world wars. Some of the larger apartment houses came later, the last in 1988. Its enviable near-downtown location and suburban character attracted families, retired people, and students who praised the neighborhood. Educational facilities met every need, from kindergarten through post-graduate years. There were attractive living spaces for virtually everyone. Little wonder realtors soon dubbed it the "Golden Triangle." How did it all come about? Neither a planned community nor the product of governmental regulations, Tuscany-Canter-

bury grew at a quick pace and became an interesting and diverse residential area, pleasing to the eye and the spirit.

In building the North Baltimore suburbs, architects followed the design styles popular at the time, and turned to Europe for inspiration and ideas. Buildings across the United States reflected the variety of architectural styles that had developed in Europe. These included the Classical or Greek Revival style favored by banks, government, and other public buildings. Homes and apartment houses adapted Gothic, Victorian, Tudor, and Georgian features as well as the International style Italian and Spanish villas. All of these are represented in the Tuscany-Canterbury neighborhood.

Detail from a c. 1922 aerial view of the Guilford and Tuscany-Canterbury area. Note the rowhouses on Canterbury and Cloverhill Roads in the background. (Jacques Kelly.)

31

George Morris built and sold the rowhouses known as University Homes, 1916–1920. They are the heart of today's neighborhood. (Baltimore Sun.)

styles on Canterbury and Cloverhill, the picturesque brick and half-timbered Tudor-esque designs on Tuscany and Ridgemede, each varying with the uneven terrain. The resulting village atmosphere has enormous visual appeal, especially in conjunction with the international and contemporary styles of the surrounding apartment buildings.

Rowhomes on Canterbury and Cloverhill

Townhouses or row homes are the core of this neighborhood. Known as University Homes, their construction began in 1916–17 and finished in 1919–20. George Morris was the realtor and builder. The architect, if not E. H. Glidden, Sr., drew inspiration from the famous designer's work on Canterbury Hall a few years earlier. Morris came to this city from Pennsylvania after the 1904 Baltimore fire believing he would find "greater opportunity in a city that needed to be rebuilt." How right he was. Living in a big house close to University Parkway, Morris immediately saw the opportunity at hand. By 1916 he had purchased the property on the west side of Charles Street Avenue. Together with others, including Major George W. Hyde, he formed the University Homes Company. In a deed dated December 20, 1917, the company sold to Morris

Of the architects active in building the neighborhood, some were born abroad or studied abroad. European-educated Edward H. Glidden designed Canterbury Hall, the icon of the neighborhood. Lawrence Hall Fowler and John Russell Pope also studied abroad. John Ahlers and Ludwig Mies van der Rohe were born in Germany. Clyde Friz, Kenneth Cameron Miller, Cyril Hebrank, and the design firms of Wyatt and Nolting, Joseph Evans Sperry and Palmer and Lamdin all possessed a fluent international vocabulary. They were familiar with the vernacular architecture of the continent and the regional variations of classical designs. This European influence shows in features such as building materials, roofing styles, arched doorways and windows, facades with French, Italian, Spanish, and Georgian characteristics—all seen in Tuscany-Canterbury. Predominating, however, are the row homes inspired by the Arts and Crafts movement in England. The cottage-

. . . a tract of land lying on the east side of Oak Street and extending from 39th Street north about six hundred and seventy feet with a depth of about two hundred and eighty feet in Baltimore Maryland which it intends to develop and improve and open up and lay out streets and lots and offer for sale the improved lots and is desirous of subjecting all of said tract of land and the said lots to certain covenants agreements easements restrictions and conditions as hereinafter set out.

This tract of land was immediately conveyed to the University Homes Company, except for two lots that Morris retained. The deed goes on to outline the restrictions, which

shall be binding upon the Company for fifty years. 1. There shall not be erected permitted maintained or operated upon any of the Land included in said tract any hospital asylum sanitorium or institution of like or kindred nature stable of any kind hog pen fowl yard or house cesspool privy vault nor any form of privy nor any manufactury nor shall any dangerous or offensive thing trade or business whatsoever be permitted or maintained on said property nor shall any live poultry hogs cattle or other livestock be Kept thereon at no time shall the land . . . be occupied by any negro or person of negro extraction this prohibition however is not intended to include the occupancy by a negro domestic servant or other person while employed. 2. . . . the Land included in said tract . . . shall be used for private residence purposes only. 3. Dwellings may be erected in groups and when erected the respective owners shall maintain their dwellings as at first erected and may not change the interior thereof into apartments nor on the exterior thereof add thereto or change the color thereof or place outbuildings or fences of any kind without the unanimous consent of the owners of the other dwellings forming the said group.

With these restrictions in place, Morris constructed expensive row homes, similar to those already finished in Guilford's Bretton Place and those on Oakenshawe, located between University Parkway and Guilford. From the eighteenth century onward, row houses have been a common domestic architectural form in Baltimore and other major eastern seaboard cities. We can only imagine why Morris built town houses rather than detached homes, as in Roland Park and Guilford. Making

The cottage style seen in these homes on Canterbury Road reflects the English Arts and Crafts movement of the early twentieth century. (Dean Wagner.)

Architect E. H. Glidden Sr. designed Canterbury Hall. (Gardens, Houses, and People, 1938.)

maximum use and profit of limited space must have been a consideration. That he was a charter member of the Commission on Government Efficiency and Economy tells us something about his character but nothing about his penchant for English-style architecture except that he was following a popular building trend. Although not as grand as the fashionable row houses built for the wealthy, nor as narrow and simple as those that housed working-class Baltimoreans, Morris's homes combined charm, good taste, and affordability. They are as attractive today as they were eighty years ago. George Morris died in 1968, at age ninety-one, in the home he built on Wendover Road.

Whether brick or stucco exterior, Tudor, English Cottage, or Colonial design, the University Homes are two and one-half stories high and thirty feet wide with a garage under the house that is accessible from the alley. The houses are grouped in threes or fours, a practice that originated in England. The interiors are spacious and gracious, generally with a center hall and open staircase, a dining room and kitchen on one side, and a living room with fireplace and sun porch on the other. The second floor has three or four bedrooms with closets and one or two bathrooms. The third floor, meant for children or for live-in servants, has one or two small bedrooms and perhaps a small bathroom. The construction throughout is solid and meant to endure. Hardwood floors and slate roofs bespeak quality as well as durability. The walls are well insulated, so rarely does one hear a sound from the adjacent house. Of outstanding importance is the fact that the homes are not dark and gloomy but flooded with light. "Sunlight Homes,"

Tuscany-Canterbury and Guilford, c. 1922. (Courtesy Jacques Kelly.)

already being built in England, had crossed the Atlantic. There are other examples of such homes throughout the city, the closest in Oakenshawe. Adaptations of English architecture were common in Baltimore after World War I.

An artist's rendering of the completed homes on Canterbury and Cloverhill appeared in the Baltimore Gas and Electric News in October 1929, touting the advantages of heating by manufactured gas. These homes were the first large group to take advantage of safe and clean gas heat as opposed to the dirt, inconvenience, and hazards of heating with coal. Moreover, heating with gas provided "the opportunity for utilization of basement space for living purposes in the home that does not require its basement to accommodate a coal bin, a storage tank and the handling of fuel and ashes." Morris apparently had a keen eye for utility and modern conveniences. Missing only the now mature old trees, the neighborhood still looks very much today as it did in 1929, characterized both then and now with varied groups of architectural styles. The gas company artist found Canterbury Road's west side empty but for the extravagant Tudor-style apartment house on the corner of 39th Street. A 1921/22 neighborhood aerial view shows Morris' house in the foreground and the Hyde mansion visible through the trees.

A retired man who grew up in the Canterbury-Cloverhill neighborhood describes the early days here:

I was brought home from the hospital, as was my sister, to the Tuscany, where my parents lived until I was four. The family then moved to Canterbury Road. Much of my early life was spent at 4000 North Charles, at

The Baltimore Gas and Electric Company advertised clean and warm basements in University Homes, a modern improvement over dirt floors and coal cellars. (Baltimore Gas and Electric News, 1929.)

University Homes, featured in the Baltimore Gas and Electric News, *1929, for their natural gas heating systems.*

"Everbright" the handsome and spacious home, belonging to my grandfather. Highfield House now occupies that site. The home was on a four-acre tract, bordering on Highfield (then Ash) and extending from Charles to Canterbury, large enough for a barn and two cows, a garden and a carriage house. My grandfather and other owners along Charles Street sold the back part of their lots to George Morris, the developer and builder of the central core of this neighborhood, Canterbury and Cloverhill Roads.

It was a large neighborhood of children, just about everybody had kids. We played in the street, played hockey on roller skates between Tuscany and Highfield on Canterbury . . . that was our hockey rink. We cut a piece of

wood about 3 inches square and that was our puck. We put a couple of bricks down and that was our goal. We played cowboys and Indians all over the place. There was lots of building going on. . . . We used to build forts down under the bridge over the Stony Run and the Ma and Pa railroad. That was our wilderness down there. The neighborhood was my whole early life.

I went to Calvert, I think starting in Kindergarten. After fourth grade, I transferred to Gilman. My parents thought that would be better for me and it was. I went with a friend who was a classmate of mine. His family had a gorgeous stone house [where the Hopkins House is now]. The chauffeur would drive us to Gilman.

Ma and Pa Railroad, 1954. (James P. Gallagher in Rudy Fischer Collection.)

The apartment house on the corner of Tuscany (the white Spanish Revival house opposite the Calvert School) was built as a one-family home. The owner used to come home from work — he had a bell in the car — and as he came toward the house he clanged the bell and the butler came out and opened the garage door. They lived pretty much to themselves . . . the[ir] kids didn't play with us much. They were very nice people. [Having a butler] was unusual. We looked upon them as wealthy. The streetcar ran along University Parkway to Roland Avenue. It went down St. Paul and all the way downtown. There were several itinerant yardmen [who worked here]. There was a house at the site of the Scottish Rite Temple. It was moved cater-corner across the street,

This Spanish Revival-style house on Tuscany Road is an example of the many architectural designs in Tuscany-Canterbury. (Dean Wagner.)

from the southwest to the northeast corner. The Guilford Manor had a drug store in the basement and later it moved to University Parkway.

A woman still living here moved to the neighborhood in 1946 as a young wife and mother to be close to Calvert School. "We were so excited to be moving uptown from Sparrows Point where my husband worked in the steel plants during the war years." Living on Cloverhill for over fifty years she has seen many changes in her family, in her home, and in her neighborhood. One thing, however, has remained constant. "There were always wonderful people on Cloverhill." She recalled the changes in the streets and alleys, in the homes, and in the neighborhood:

Charles Street changed from a street of big houses and with wraparound porches and one apartment house, the Warrington, to a street with all apartment houses. Now Cloverhill is a very attractive street, it wasn't when we came. . . . The landscaping has made a great difference. Over the years, the alley (which

used to be called a lane) has changed even more dramatically. It changed from ash cans and garbage cans, and clotheslines to beautified . . . the decks have added interest. The ground was awful as far as planting things to grow. . . . [Decks have] improved the looks and made a nice outdoor area, covering up the bricks, messy grass, wire fences; there was a need for [decks]. I remember the first porch built in the backyard and it was wonderful, safe, dark, no floodlights, just like being in the country. You could see the stars. The gingko trees in the alley are the original trees, wonderful trees, very ancient.

The Morrises [George Morris, the builder-developer] lived on Canterbury. During the war years, he gave the land between the east side of Canterbury and University Parkway for victory gardens. And when the war ended, he gave it to the children for a baseball field. The activities for children were wonderful . . . When my children were little they would run to the window to see the lamplighter. Waiting for him was a big event. Christmas caroling was a wonderful tradition, we went all over the neighborhood. That went on for years. I did all my Christmas shopping in the Ambassador [gift shop] and had my hair done in the beauty parlor, and the drug store was right down the hall. That was a great advantage in this neighborhood. . . . He [Mr. Mullan, the builder of the Ambassador] gave the shops to members of his family.

I was heartbroken when they built the apartments on Oak Place (now 4300 North Charles); that was twenty years ago. That was a big area, it was all deep woods that went all the way down to Linkwood. There were springs behind the Cathedral and the water was piped under Charles Street to Oak Place. There is water down there now and not long ago my husband saw a blue heron. I remember when a deer [from the wood] was killed on Charles Street twenty-five or thirty years ago. We were all distressed when they built the apartments. That brought more cars and more danger for the children.

Most of these houses have been renovated, updating bathrooms and kitchens. What was missing in this house was a coat closet and a downstairs lavatory. We took a pantry and split it and put in a darling lavatory. We are using the back hallway with peg hangers for what we wear every day. In the master bedroom there were two "buzz buttons" and a box in the kitchen to call a servant when needed.

This recounting of the early days of this community illustrates how different the neighborhood is now from when it was developed.

Gaslights were installed in our neighborhood as the houses were built along Charles Street and throughout the community. The lamplighter lit the lamps every night, riding around in a horse-drawn carriage carrying a ladder. The ladder rested against the rack at the top of the light pole as he lit the flame.

Today we see the forty new and handsome electric streetlights installed on Cloverhill, Canterbury, and Tuscany Roads that replaced the gaslight in the 1950s. When the original cast-iron, one-piece poles were replaced with poles accommodating electricity, the originals were sold to the Disney Company. They now adorn Main Street in Disney World, Florida. Baltimore City had the first street lighting in the United States, when gaslights appeared in 1817, a development commemorated by a plaque at Baltimore and Holliday Streets.

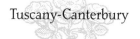

The Rowhomes on Ridgemede, Tuscany, and Tuscany Court

The construction of the next section of our neighborhood began at the end of the 1920s. Land records for the Tuscany/Ridgemede section of the community show frequent changes of ownership, a local reflection of the national nervousness about investment in land and the slow-down in construction that preceded the Great Depression. Without records explaining the ten-year time difference in building the western section of the neighborhood, as

Young families moved into the homes on Cloverhill Road. Many stayed for decades and raised their families. (Baltimore Gas and Electric News, 1929.)

Long-time residents remember the lamplighter, 1947. (Maryland Historical Society.)

and Tuscany, on the other hand, posed an engineering problem. The houses would have to be built to conform to the slopes and hills, or the land would have to be leveled. Fortunately, the developers and builders followed the Roland Park Company's example and Frederick Law Olmsted's design theory, and built with respect for the land as it is.

The Robinson and Slagle Company purchased a sizable tract in the area and began construction of the Tuscany and Ridgemede houses in 1928. They built the first four houses at the Tuscany-Ridgemede intersection and three more at the bottom of Tuscany Road. The company went bankrupt and the Mullan Contracting Company took over the work, probably in 1930. The Mullans built the rest of the houses on Tuscany and Ridgemede Roads and those on Tuscany Court. The company is still in operation, but they unfortunately have disposed of all the records pertaining to that period.

A member of the family who bought the very first house on Tuscany Road now lives in his family home. He recalls his child-hood in rich detail:

compared to the eastern section, it is reasonable to advance differences in topography as an explanation. Canterbury and Cloverhill were on level ground and very close to transportation. Ridgemede

Tuscany Court, c. 1940. The Mullan Contracting Company took over the bankrupt Robinson and Slagle Company in 1930 and finished the work. (Private Collection.)

My parents purchased our house in 1929. We moved in on July 1. It was the first house to be occupied in this part of the neighborhood. We were not alone for long; other families moved in on July 2 and July 3. The only finished houses in 1929 were two groups of four, a group on each side of Ridgemede Road at Tuscany Road. I lived here throughout my childhood, and after pursuing my graduate education and my career elsewhere, I returned in 1977. But this was always my home.

My parents moved here with their five children because they liked the area. I remember it was a wonderful place to grow up. Across the street and all the way down to Tuscany Court was open woods. About one-third of the woods was enclosed by a rustic fence; the fence we see today came later. At one point there was a racquet court in the woods, but it was removed after fire damage.

I have fond memories of the Maryland Casualty Company chimes, and of the Ma and Pa Railroad which ran along the Stony Run. There were few automobiles then, but plenty of delivery trucks for milk, bread, laundry, and dry cleaning, for ice for the icebox (brought by a horse-drawn cart), for coal for the coal-fired furnace, for the ashes, and for most department stores.

I remember Mr. Thomas Mullan Sr. walking around the neighborhood, soliciting approval of the residents for building the Ridgemede Apartments. He built that apartment house so it would fit in with the neighborhood. He was sensitive to the concerns of the homeowners about preserving the architectural integrity and the residential character of the neigh-borhood. I saw the apartment being built on Ridgemede Road, and the houses on Tuscany and Ridgemede and on Tuscany Court.

A resident on Ridgemede describes the houses, and her own house:

Contractor Thomas Mullan, n.d. (Louise Flanigan.)

Each townhouse on Ridgemede is different from the others. However, each house has certain features in common: panes of Venetian glass in leaded casement windows; a fireplace in an inglenook; living rooms extensively paneled in pine and some other hardwood; fine architectural details — brass light switches (each tipped with a small round glove that glows in the dark), wrought-iron door knobs, interesting stone and brickwork, slate roofs, handsome wood trim.

Our house, the largest I believe, has an enclosed front porch, entrance hall, and coat closet with a sink, a spacious dining room, a sunroom, a butler's pantry with a broom closet, and a kitchen with a separate pantry. The kitchen opens onto a small stone porch with an iron railing and a deck.

On the second floor there is a master bedroom with a fireplace, a dressing room, four closets, and a bathroom; two other roomy bedrooms, a second bathroom, a large linen closet and a broom closet. On the third floor there are two bedrooms, a full bath and a half

41

The Ridgemede
Apartments, c. 1950.
(Private Collection.)

*bath and three large storage closets, one
cedar-lined. The basement has a finished room
with a stone fireplace, a marvelous stained
glass ship in the door to the laundry room and
unusual panes of ornamental glass in the
above ground windows.*

Who designed these attractive houses?
The answer appeared to be lost to history,
for architects are not usually included in
public records such as deeds and builders
do not typically keep such information
about ordinary residences. But a search for
building permits yielded the answer. The
Daily Record, a business journal established
in 1908, published the name of the builder
and the architect as part of the building
permit. Two of these permits, dated

November 29, 1928, establish John Ahlers
as the architect of the Tuscany and Ridgemede row houses located at 213–215
Tuscany Road and 201–203 Ridgemede
Road:

*Robinson and Slagle, Inc., two two-and-one-
half-story brick dwellings, 213–215 Tuscany
Road; slate and Carey roofs; hot water heat;
cost $13,000. John Ahlers, architect; owner,
builder.*

Because of the similarity in architectural
style, it is reasonable to attribute all of the
row houses on Tuscany and Ridgemede to
John Ahlers. An account of his work in *The
Townsman* of 1928 stated that the "Tuscany
. . . development" was his first major

42

assignment after he left the Joseph Evans Sperry firm. Ahlers continued his work on these houses after the Mullan Company took over the building project. The success of the Tuscany plan brought Ahlers the opportunity to work with the Roland Park Company, where he was associated with the design team of Palmer and Lamdin. His major achievement with the Roland Park Company was the design for Original Northwood. It was his ambition "to plan a development of houses within the reach of the low-salaried white collar worker." Mary Ellen Hayward describes the houses on Tuscany Road and in Northwood as "the row houses in Baltimore which use materials and space in unusual and creative ways." Ahlers later designed homes for individuals in addition to public buildings—Loyola at Blakefield is a notable example. In 1930 he won the Society of Beaux-Arts Architects' National Architectural Design Medal for a gothic cathedral that was never constructed.

When Ahlers turned his attention to Northwood, Tuscany Road was not yet completed. Mullan employed architect Cyril Hebrank to finish the houses and retained Ahlers' Tudor designs. So successful was the entire development that *Gardens, Houses and People,* in the September, 1938 issue described Tuscany as "an ideal place to live" This article, filled with interesting details, is reprinted in the Appendix.

Tuscany Court is a small circle of Colonial- and Tudor-style houses, constructed by the Mullan Company after Robinson and Slagle sold them the land in 1929. The deed contained one proviso that the construction of the row homes must be accomplished so that there was "no interference with light and air." Does this provision suggest the presence of some opposition to building the more modest structures in a limited space? Neighbor-

Washing System used by the Roland Park Company on University Parkway, October 6, 1906. (Maryland Historical Society.)

hood lore has it that Guilford residents opposed the Tuscany Court houses which were nonetheless built in the 1940s. The brick, fieldstone, and half-timber exteriors, the varied terrain, porches, terraces, and front-yard gardens make the court an

John Ahlers, n.d. (Dean Wagner.)

The oldest house in Tuscany-Canterbury dates to 1892. (Private Collection.)

attractive and appealing niche within the neighborhood. Comparison with row-homes in Homeland indicates that the architect may have been Kenneth Cameron Miller.

A professor at Hopkins purchased the first house on Tuscany Court in November, 1945. He lived there until 1977, moving then to the Ambassador for his final years. A tall, formal man, he was devoted to

Hopkins and to the Faculty Club, where he walked daily for lunch and dinner. One of his reasons for living here was to be close to the university and to the Faculty Club.

One resident of the court since 1960 moved back to Baltimore because it was her childhood home. "As a widowed mother of two, I wanted a home I could maintain. It's very quiet and private. Where else in Baltimore would I have these wonderful trees? It's my own little plantation. And the people are so nice — many professors."

The Detached Homes

Several of the sixteen detached residences in Tuscany-Canterbury merit description. One because it is the oldest structure in the neighborhood and others for their architecture. On West Highfield Road, wedged behind the Winthrop House condominiums, the oldest house easily escapes notice. But look again and there it is, a tall, narrow, Victorian cottage, situated in a pleasant yard with tall trees in the background. At the back of the yard and down a slope is the stream that comes under Charles Street, surfaces briefly and then disappears under the Calvert School playing field as it makes its way to the Stony Run. Herons nest along the tiny stream in that small, wooded glen, a fitting setting for our only surviving 1890s house. Through the land records, we can trace the lot on which the house was built back to 1892. It had earlier belonged to the Merryman family. Tracing the exact boundaries of a specific property can be quite challenging. Surveyors measured the tract according to the available landmarks and early deeds note trees, stumps (yes, stumps), fences, and other property lines as boundary markers that have long-since disappeared. The deed reproduced here probably includes the property on which

the oldest house in Tuscany-Canterbury stands. There is no clear evidence of when the house was built. Other buildings from that era are long since gone, surviving only on old maps and in our imaginations. Here is a description of the interior by the current occupant:

This three-story, full basement Victorian frame house is apparently 101 years old. We found a newspaper with the date 1898 stuffed into the wall as insulation. The house is fourteen feet wide and about forty-five feet long, with an "L" shaped porch.

The house went through several remodelings in the seventy-five years before we bought it in 1975. The original kitchen was most likely the current dining room, [and when we bought it] the kitchen and the second floor bathroom had apparently been back porches. The kitchen was thirteen feet long, four feet deep, with no counter or storage space. The original toilet facilities were . . . an outhouse? [The city sewer line was extended to the house in 1913.]

We have remodeled several times. With the help of a neighborhood architect, we moved the front entrance back to permit a center hall with powder room and coat closet, and increased the depth of the kitchen to seven feet. Later we turned the attic into a study, adding a small bathroom, removed a second-story deck to enlarge the bathroom, added a rear deck and designed a stair tower and an additional room and deck at the back of the third floor.

What was once a very small house has been transformed into a comfortable family home that still maintains its Victorian character.

Lawrence Hall Fowler, one of the most well-known and prominent architects in Baltimore in the first half of the twentieth century, designed five Tuscany-Canterbury

Lawrence Hall Fowler, n.d. The architect designed five Tuscany-Canterbury houses and the Calvert School. (The Ferdinand Hamburger Archives of the Johns Hopkins University.)

houses and the Calvert School. Fowler received his training in New York City at Columbia University and in Paris at the Ècole des Beaux-Arts. His "eclectic" style, as it is described by an admirer, may be the product of his varied and intercontinental background. The style of his designs certainly varies to fit the site and "to fit the wishes of his patron," but always was

"refined" with great attention to detail, both outside and inside, even to selecting the furniture. His awareness of the relationship between building materials and design is rightly praised. Two of the five Fowler houses in the neighborhood have been torn down, one on 39th Street, built in 1911, to make way for a parking lot, and one on Oak Place to make way for apartment houses.

Of Fowler's three surviving houses, he built one on Highfield Road, in 1925 for his own residence. The house is close to the road, but surrounded by a jungle of trees, bushes, and greenery that ends in the little stream that separates Highfield Road from Oak Place. The French eclectic exterior is simple and without ornamentation, almost modern in conception. The multi-level interior, with its interesting use of space and materials, is utterly delightful. It is a house with which one falls in love.

When Fowler lived in his house on Highfield Road he was in the midst of a cluster of his own creations, two on Oak Place and one on Tuscany Road, as well as

Fowler's home on Highfield Road, 1925. (Dawn Reiken.)

Courtyard at One Oak Place, n.d. (The John Work Garrett Library of the Johns Hopkins University.)

the Calvert School. One Oak Place is especially grand. He designed and constructed it for his sisters, one of whom, Alice, was the headmistress of St. Timothy's School. She must have ruled the school with a will of steel, judging from the correspondence about construction between brother and sister. He addressed her as "My dear Miss Fowler." "I had to decide about the bricks in great fear," he told her in one letter. "The other samples with less color were very poor indeed, so after much inquiry I selected the oil finish as giving nearest the effect you want." She replied, "My dear Mr. Fowler," and complained about various expenses, especially the cost of the bricks. We do not know if Miss Fowler liked the finished house but it is certainly an exceptional single-family home. Georgian Revival in design, the exterior has fine proportions and wonderfully detailed brickwork. The interior is

replete with spacious rooms, elegant moldings, lovely windows facing the woods and stream, and a Waterford crystal chandelier. The country atmosphere of open space and the feeling of leisurely and gracious living are still visible despite the construction of the "4300" apartments. In 1916 it must have been like living on a splendid country estate, far removed from the steamy and smelly city. With eight servants and a chauffeur, all living on the premises, the Misses Fowler surely lived an indulged life.

Since those early days, Oak Place has had several owners, the last one converting it into five apartments that are now part of the 4300 apartment complex. The current resident of the servants' quarters on the top floor has this to say about living there:

Bolton Hill was becoming too dangerous for me; somebody put a gun in my face and then

47

Building Castalia, 1929, right and below. (Calvert School Archives.)

my neighbor was raped. So I began looking for an apartment in a big, old house in Roland Park. When I saw 4300, I wanted to be here, but they had a long waiting list. The apartments were wonderfully designed, with big rooms, nice kitchens, lots of closets. The owner loved animals, and I had two cats. Then the owner told me [he] had a very old apartment, difficult to rent because it was on the third floor, with narrow steps and it wasn't renovated. I fell in love with it immediately, and that was fifteen years ago. I don't want to live anywhere else, this is where I want to die. You hear nothing but birds, the rustling of the trees and the sound of the brook.

When the house was built, this was the servants' living quarters. There was a long hall, with eight bedrooms, one for each servant. The chauffer lived in the garage. Two of the bedrooms are now one room and that is my living room. I have a bedroom, a guest room, a very big study which was the butler's bedroom, a kitchen, a laundry room, a bathroom, and two wonderful, huge storage rooms. I use one to dry my laundry, summer and winter. The feeling of these rooms is like a country house in France, sloping ceilings, *dormer windows, odd little and not-so-little rooms. The first and second floor apartments are more formal and elegant. The whole area is incredibly peaceful. Once I woke up to see a little family of baby foxes rolling around in the garden, like puppies. Some people wanted to keep the fox family, but others wanted them taken away. My neighbor's cat, tough and intrepid, faced down the fox, and they got to be buddies, sleeping in the sun on the drive-way! But eventually the foxes disappeared.*

Around the corner on Tuscany Road is quite another Fowler home, an elegant, dig-nified castle, multi-leveled, of heavy field-stone construction. The tall, narrow win-dows on the front façade and the roofline are Tudor Revival in conception. The trees and the garden with two ponds fed by natural springs also convey the sense of Classical antiquity dear to the heart of Virgil Hillyer, first headmaster of Calvert School, for whom Fowler built the house in 1929. It was Hillyer who gave the house its name, Castalia, after the spring on Mount Parnassus where the Muses met for inspira-tion.

Across the street from the Calvert School is a fine Italianate house, built for Jesse Benesch, a purveyor of modern furniture. This house, built in 1924 or 1925, sits in a spacious garden. It belonged to a family of means, with servants, a butler, and a whole room for the Skinner pipe organ, later donated to the Christ Lutheran Church on Sollers Point Road. They sold the house in 1960 to the Hurlock family, who then converted it into six apartments. The architectural style of the house is Spanish Eclectic, reminiscent of Clyde Friz's Garden Apartments across the way, but the name of the architect is not known. Frank Benjamin is a reasonable guess.

Two other homes that capture interest are located on Linkwood Road. One, between Ridgemede and Stoneyford Road, is built on a rocky cliff that was once the site of the Paradise Mill on the Stony Run. The house, built in 1956 on land purchased from Clyde Friz (who developed the Tuscany, the Lombardy, and the Gardens of Guilford), has remained in the same family to this day. The yard originally contained drying ponds for sewage before Linkwood

Lawrence Hall Fowler built Castalia for Virgil Hillyer, first headmaster of the Calvert School, in 1929. (Calvert School Archives.)

49

Road opened. The sewage disappeared long ago, but the ponds were filled in only recently. The architect for this unusual hillside lot was Frazier Baldwin, who put the front door on the side of the house facing the gardens that surround the Tuscany Apartments. In recent years, a terraced addition has been added.

A present-day member of the original family recalls times gone by:

I have lived here for fifty-six years, in the house my parents built in 1936. The lots were bought from Clyde Friz. It was a multi-level lot, and the house is built on a rocky cliff. The lot was [the site] of an old sawmill. Joseph Coale, who works for Crown Petroleum, has a picture of the mill. Before Linkwood Road was put in there were drying ponds for sewage [on the lot]. The stream was redirected when Linkwood was opened.

Three streams once came into the Stony Run. The Homeland Stream comes through Evergreen and tunnels under Charles Street to north of Cold Spring Lane, another between my house and the Tuscany apartments is tunneled to the Stony Run, and the stream (near Oak Place) is tunneled under the Calvert playing field and tunneled down to Stony Run. When I was a boy I used to crawl up one of those tunnels quite a way.

Where the Ridgewood is was an open field until the late 1950s and that was a great place for children to play. The entire neighborhood was a playground for the children — the open lots, the Stony Run, the gardens where the Colonnade is now. Through the 1950s, the Ma and Pa Railroad ran along the Stony Run. Closing the Ma and Pa cut off the vagrants and eliminated the trash because people used to dump [everything] there.

The neighborhood boundaries use to include all of Warrenton Road, at least this [the south] side, and none of Charles Street. Guilford said Charles Street on the west was turning commercial, so they gave Charles Street West to Tuscany-Canterbury, and we gave them Warrenton. [The Guilford Association has no record of this transaction.]

Also, at the foot of Tuscany Road, is an enormous fieldstone and stucco, half-timbered house, originally for two families that Clyde Friz designed and built for himself and his daughter. At one time it was the home of well-known Baltimore artist Don Swann. In recent years, it has been redesigned as a single-family home.

Several other detached residences have been altered to accommodate several apartments. One is the attractive Colonial Revival house on Stony Run Lane.

The Apartment Buildings

There are twenty-four apartment and condominium buildings in Tuscany-Canterbury. This figure does not include the handful of single-family houses that have been converted to multiple-person dwellings. These apartments resemble canyon walls along Charles Street, University Parkway, and 39th Street and present an imposing facade to the world. Along Charles Street the apartments have replaced the mansions built in the 1880s and 1890s and the rest were built on vacant land.

From 1912 to 1925

The first apartment building in Tuscany-Canterbury, Canterbury Hall, was built before World War I on the corner of Canterbury Road and 39th Street. George Morris constructed the extravagant Tudor building in 1912 and architect Edward H. Glidden Sr. designed it. The structure is "built like a bomb shelter," with walls so thick that three weeks instead of three days were required to put in cable for television.

Architect Edward H. Glidden designed the Hamlyn in the late 1920s. (Dean Wagner.)

Special drill bits had to be obtained to get through walls eighteen inches thick. The building has fifteen apartments on three and one-half floors, each one different from the others and each with a gas fireplace. Three smaller apartment buildings (now condominiums)—the Lincoln, the Hamilton, and the Hamlyn—went up at the same intersection in the late 1920s. Architect Frederick E. Beall designed the first of these homes, built for John L. Robinson in 1925. Glidden designed the Hamlyn and the Hamilton. It is this cluster of four apartments that constitute the Canterbury Square buildings. Guilford Manor, a short distance away on University Parkway, was constructed in 1919 in a Federal Revival style.

Farther up Canterbury Road is the Dundee (now condominiums), built in 1921 and designed by Edward L. Palmer of the architectural firm Palmer, Willis, and Lambdin. The residences are unusually spacious. Each unit has a large kitchen, dining room, living room with fireplace, den, two bedrooms, two baths, and high ceilings with crown moldings. Each condominium also has a porch and a garage. The nearby Berkeley House, built in about 1920 is an attractive Italian Renaissance building with equally spacious condominiums, but no porches.

Two apartment houses on University Parkway, 104 West and 106 West were built on property purchased from George Morris. 104 West claims to be the oldest property on the block, dating from 1914, and 106 West followed in 1920. Both are elegant Italian Renaissance structures.

During and soon after World War I, builder and architect Clyde Friz constructed three apartment houses on part of the land he had purchased from the University Parkway Company in 1913. He built the

51

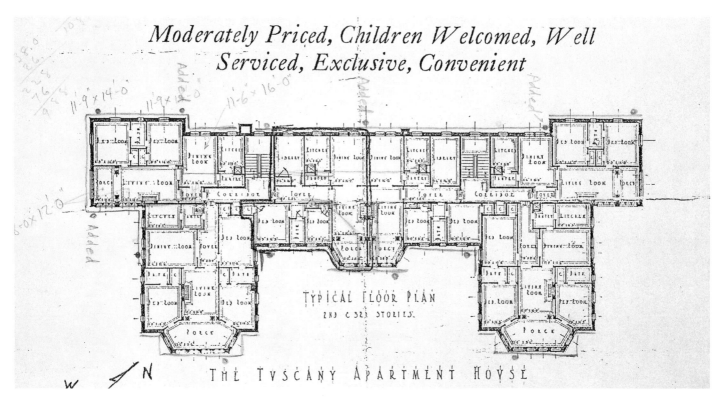

Moderately Priced, Children Welcomed, Well Serviced, Exclusive, Convenient

TYPICAL FLOOR PLAN
2ND & 3RD STORIES.

THE TUSCANY APARTMENT HOUSE

W · N

The Tuscany Cooperative, 1915, utilized the popular open court design pictured on the right. (Architectural Record, 1921.)

Lombardy in 1915, the Tuscany in 1918, and the Gardens Apartments (now known as the Gardens of Guilford) in 1922. Situated in a secluded, almost hidden enclave of the neighborhood, the Tuscany and the Lombardy, both cooperative apartments, are handsome Italian Renaissance buildings. The Spanish Eclectic Gardens of Guilford condominiums are distinctly Mediterranean in appearance.

The Tuscany utilized the "open court" design that developed as apartment houses appeared in the suburbs, where space was plentiful and land relatively less expensive. In contrast to the block-like designs used in the crowded cities, Friz designed a shallow building on the edges of a square with the front, or court, open to the street. The *Architectural Record* of 1921 describes the Tuscany as "Perhaps the best example of the wide and shallow lot treatment." These lovely designs were abandoned as land prices increased in value. The Carolina apartments on University Parkway also follow the open-court design.

Theodore Wells Pietsch designed the 1923 building.

A former resident of the Gardens apartments describes the plantings she placed around the buildings. A photographer and psychoanalyst—as well as a gardener—she moved to the location in 1950 and stayed for seventeen years:

It was a wonderful place to have an office and a dog. I got into trees first, identifying them because I was going to the Adirondacks then. My description of how I got into gardening was published in Horticulture, *June, 1970.*

I became the gardener of the Gardens Apartments quite by accident. During the nine years of the garden's growth, it became a rescue mission in several ways. Now in its young maturity it gives pleasure to many who know nothing of its beginnings. Newcomers sit on benches in the little European garden under the central elm. Children play in the sand at their feet.

Neighbors detour through our cul-de-sac to enjoy the azaleas blooming in the spring, to

52

survey the progress of the Japanese garden on the hill. . . . The garden means most to us who have been rescued by it, who have participated in the transplanting of many plants from their endangered homes. . . . Ten years ago one of the great bonuses of acquiring my first large dog was a Sunday walk in the neighboring park-like area. . . . [In] the spring of 1961, I noticed that one marshy area was growing smaller by the week. Men were filling it with soil from the excavation for a high-rise apartment. At the edge of the marsh was blooming a mass of bloodroot, some with double blossoms. Though I had no gardening experience, it seemed sensible to try to save a few of the plants. . . . I maneuvered the treasures across the stream to the car. A week later the marsh was gone, buried beneath a bed of clay.

Behind the apartment building where I lived was a strip of wasteland almost two hundred feet long, rising twenty-five feet . . . to the alley above. It was treed primarily with locusts, a few oaks, hickory, wild cherry and sassafras, and the earth was solid clay. . . . Scooping out large holes in the clay I planted the bloodroot in its own soil where I could keep an eye on it. As the plants survived and grew, so did my interest and enthusiasm. [Before long] rescued violets, Solomon's seal, Jack-in-the-pulpits, and wild geranium enlarged the area of cultivation.

The long bank became a series of wild gardens, a barren circle of earth under three red cedars is now green with Rhododendron fortunei. . . . a little European garden [was] created from a dust bowl . . . [under] a large American elm. Now it is a pleasure to sit in the garden, to visit with neighbors or to look up to the natural chapel whose frescoes perpetually change.

To build this garden, she rescued plants from near and far and nurtured them to

Tuscany-Canterbury

The Tuscany Cooperative, 1915. (Architectural Record, 1921.)

53

grow and bloom. She purchased many others and gathered hundreds of different varieties of trees, bushes, and flowers. Many young boys, introduced to her by her house-keeper, helped with this project [over the] years. She taught them and encouraged them, and, in time, "The boys have grown into men and have moved on to their own lives . . . carrying with them the love and spirit of the out-of-doors." When the Gardens apartments were sold and turned into condominiums, she moved on and created another garden around her new abode, rescuing an occasional plant from her first garden.

From 1925 to World War II

The Gardens of Guilford, 1927. (Maryland Historical Society.)

The construction of apartments along Charles Street and University Parkway con-

tinued during the 1920s and 1930s, ceased during the Second World War, and then resumed. The last of them, the Colonnade, was built in 1988. The Winthrop House, the Highfield House, the Warrington, and the Cambridge all replaced the grand mansions built in the 1880s. The War-rington, Georgian Revival in design, was one of the first, replacing the Hyde mansion and rivaling it in magnificence. Advertised in the Sun in 1927 as the first of the "exclu-sive New York type," the designers, Wyatt and Nolting described the twelve-story building as having:

four suites on each floor. Each will contain an entrance hall, living room, library, dining room, pantry, kitchen, and four master bedrooms, each connecting with a bath. There will be a servant's hall, two servants' bed-

rooms and bath. The dining and living rooms will have wood-burning open fireplaces. There will be two duplex apartments on the roof, with private roof gardens. . . . [They] will represent an investment of $1,400,000 when completed.

We can imagine the delight with which people moved from the downtown, with its congestion, noise, and foul air to the sylvan pleasures of the suburbs in 1927. Today the escape from the city extends all the way to, and into, Pennsylvania. One resident of thirty-six years mourns the changes she has experienced in this neighborhood since the 1960s:

Charles Street used to have big houses with stables and garages in back, with quarters for the chauffeur above. In the old days there were lots of big cars and chauffeurs. We used to have Junior League meetings in the building behind the house on the corner of High-field. When they took down the garages behind the Charles Street houses, there were rats all over the place. We had a terrible time getting rid of them. The apartment houses now on Charles Street shut out the light and you don't have the sunrises we used to have.

At about the same time another Wyatt and Nolting Georgian Revival design was built on University Parkway on the "last parcel of Merryman's Lott still owned by a family member." The year was 1926, and the owner was Mrs. Henry Lucas, née Merryman, who lived to be over ninety. Promoted as a "$1,000,000 apartment building," with seventy-four suites, it was named 100 University Parkway West. Its T-shape is embellished with garden courts on each side. One court leads to the hand-some entrance on University Parkway that is, unfortunately, rarely used and a more utilitarian access is at the side. The other

garden court, facing the side of the First Church of Christ, Scientist has been bricked up over several floors, a sad and unattractive sight. This sturdy dowager of apartments now overlooks the expanded Hopkins athletic field with its infelicitous wall along University Parkway in one direction and the rear courtyard of the Colonnade in the other.

Doorway at the Gardens of Guilford, c. 1980. (Barbara Young.)

100 West, c. 1926. (Private Collection.)

interior decor is quite at odds with the building and the neighborhood. The spare, exposed, building materials and duct work give it an industrial or architecture brut ambiance. The vivid pumpkin, curry, and paprika color scheme, the wild paintings on the walls, and the cheery young staff warm an otherwise stark appearance. The food is exclusively vegetarian, espousing "a healthy lifestyle, offering alternatives to support healthy eating and drinking." As the only casual café in the area, it is already a success with Hopkins and Loyola students, and with those who want a quick bite but not fast food.

For many years, the University Parkway Pharmacy, originally a drugstore in the basement of Guilford Manor, was a much loved and utilized shop at 100 West. The location is now the home of a vegetarian restaurant, the One World Café. The

Nearby on Canterbury Road is the Ambassador, a dignified and elegant structure of Halls-of-Ivy Tudor/Gothic design, oozing good taste and tradition. It was built by the Mullan Company in 1930, the same company that built the Ridgemede and Tuscany Tudor homes. Although each project employed a different architect

Floor plan, 100 West, 1926. (Private Collection.)

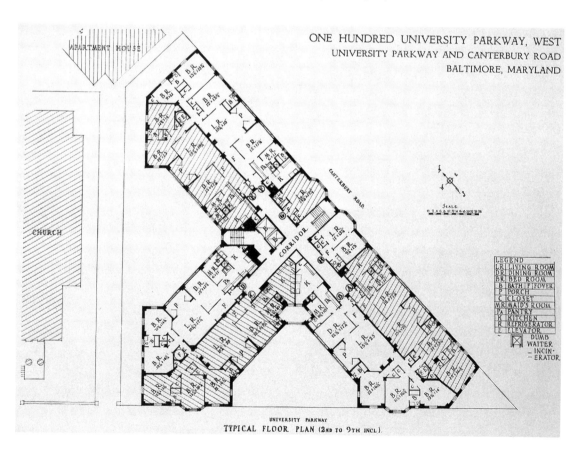

ONE HUNDRED UNIVERSITY PARKWAY, WEST
UNIVERSITY PARKWAY AND CANTERBURY ROAD
BALTIMORE, MARYLAND

TYPICAL FLOOR PLAN (2ND TO 9TH INCL.)

(Louis Roulou of Washington, D.C., for the Ambassador), the quality of construction and attention to detail is evident in both. The placement of the Ambassador, back from the street, with a well-tended lawn and plantings, provides a very agreeable setting for this fine building. Only 20 percent of the lot is used for the structure and the entrance is just behind a handsome portico. At the rear of the building is a lovely garden constructed on the roof of the garage, which is partially underground. The garden is accessible from the attractive dining room and greatly appreciated by the patrons. It has had many cuisine transformations over the years and currently serves a highly recommended Indian fare. Access to the dining room is through the spacious lobby, adorned with fireplace, diamond-pane windows of leaded glass embellished with Venetian glass coats of arms, and a decorated ceiling.

Included in the construction of the building were several shops, the principal one a gift shop for the builder's daughter, Louise Mullan Flanigan, who made it her domain for many years. Mrs. Flanigan recalls those years with great affection:

I just loved it, picking out things for people . . . We had very loyal customers, sometimes for three generations. I was there for sixty years [from 1934 to 1994]. In the summer I could travel, see the world. I've been around it five times, to the Antarctic and to the North Pole.

Various shops have come and gone since then, but none has equaled Mrs. Flanigan's record. The former gift shop currently houses a flower shop.

The Northway, a "Neo-Colonial" ziggurat built on spacious grounds in 1932, featured large apartments, elaborately decorated public rooms, and many amenities for the residents. Now, almost seventy years later

The Ambassador, c. 1930. (Louise Flanigan.)

Louise Mullan Flanigan, the builder's daughter, operated a gift shop in the Ambassador. (Louise Flanigan.)

the building is the victim of relative neglect and a transient student population. The building shows its age, but plans are underway to restore the Northway. It will undergo "subtractive renovation and restoration."

The last apartment house built before the onset of World War II was the Ridgemede, another product of the Mullan Contracting Company. Completed in 1940, it is Tudor

Tuscany-Canterbury as shown on the Sanborn Fire Insurance map. (Insurance Maps of Baltimore, Maryland [New York: Sanborn Map Company, 1938/1958].)

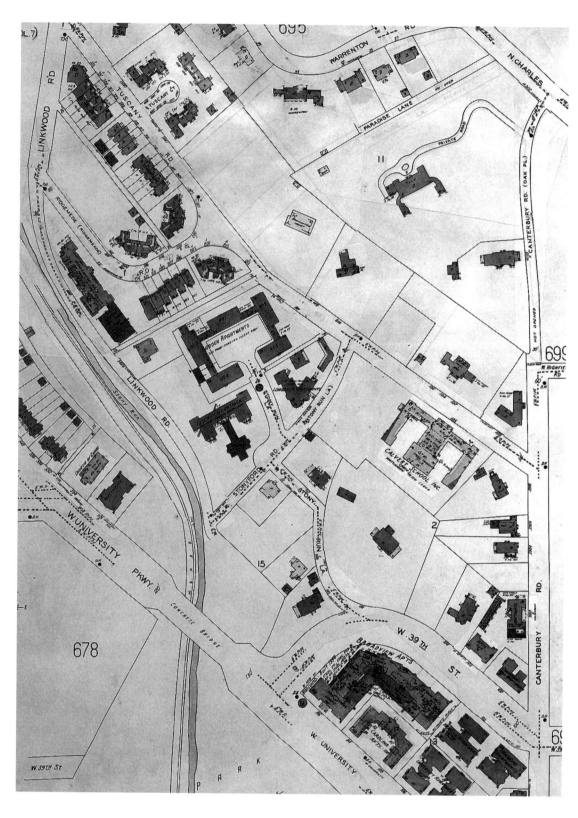

in conception, like the houses on Ridgemede. Placed on a narrow lot, the building is long and low and follows the slope of the hill down toward Linkwood. Apparently Mr. Mullan puzzled about the use of this hillside site. His daughter reported that he came home one day and announced, "I think I have an answer for the hillside [property]; it will fit in on the hillside [to] go in on the third floor, and up two flights

58

and down two flights." It was a happy solution, for the building does not overpower the two- and three-story houses around it. The half-timbering is especially nice. As with the Ambassador, Mullan sited the building so as to provide space for trees and a garden all around the building. The "secret garden," as it is called by the residents, is accessible by a locked gate. Picturesque stone walls and staircases, lush roses and other perennials, and a boxwood border rest on the roof of the garage, gained from a hidden driveway. The residents care for the garden.

In 1966 a companion apartment house, the Ridgewood, was built on the opposite side of the street and followed the same down-the-hill design idea. Less elegant than the Ridgemede, it nonetheless fits in with the rest of the neighborhood. When one's principle view is of the back of the Ridgewood, the wish for more architectural creativity in rear facades is more than an idle whim. Sadly, Mullan's ingenuity failed here.

We should pause here in our description of the growth of the apartment buildings and look at the neighborhood as depicted on a map. The Sanborn Fire Insurance Maps, begun in 1867, provide a wonderful snapshot overview of the built environment of more than 12,000 cities at successive intervals, mainly in the early twentieth century. Baltimore City maps were published between 1890 and 1982. Sanborn devised his maps because fire was an enormous peril to cities before and into the twentieth century. He was an employee of the Aetna Insurance Company in Connecticut where he saw the opportunity for a business of his own and seized it. Visual accuracy and detailed information about the size, composition and location of every building proved to be useful to insurance companies to calculate risks and liabilities.

For anyone unfamiliar with the devastating effect of a rampant fire in a city, Sherry Olson's *Baltimore, The Building of an American City*, contains a vivid description of the great Baltimore fire of 1904 on the environment and the economy. She does not mention the Sanborn maps in her discussion of the insurance tangles and rebuilding efforts; however, one can imagine their utility.

Happily, Tuscany-Canterbury has escaped the devastation of fires (except for the predecessor of the St. James). Historians, architects, anthropologists, genealogists, and others interested in the growth and development of cities now prize these maps. We turn to them for that purpose. By looking at the maps of 1938 and 1958, we can literally see ourselves growing. Their clarity is such that the old adage is apt — one picture is worth a thousand words.

The Broadview Apartments, 1950. (Maryland Historical Society.)

After World War II

John K. Ruff built the Broadview Apartments in 1950 as a source of financial support for his several daughters and the project answered a growing community need for long- and short-term rentals. Conveniently located on University Parkway, its 465 units of varying size provide comfortable domiciles for working adults, students, retired individuals, and visitors to the university. Also in the Broadview is Jeannier's, an unpretentious restaurant with fine French cuisine. It has earned, and deserves, its appellation as one of "Baltimore's Best."

Woodcliff Manor, also part of the Broadview, sits across the street and is an unobtrusive group of garden apartments with a 1950s appearance. These apartments are located on the site of Woodcliffe, the country house of Richard Capron who was active in developing Roland Park. In 1944 he sold the house to The Johns Hopkins University. The building housed four of the university's presidents, Isaiah Bowman, Detlev Bronk, Lowell Reed and Milton Eisenhower. When President Eisenhower refused to continue living there, Woodcliffe was sold, demolished, and replaced by the garden apartments. An adjacent property, originally part of Capron's Woodcliffe estate, also contained a magnificent house, owned for a time by John C. Legg. After his death in 1963, the house was demolished and replaced by Hopkins House.

The Broadview created quite a stir in the neighborhood when its owners sought to build a parking lot on 39th Street by replacing Ascot House, a Lawrence Hall

Lawrence Fowler's Ascot House, 1911, demolished in the mid-1980s for a Broadview parking lot. (The John Work Garrett Library of the Johns Hopkins University.)

Fowler building dating from the early 1900s. The Broadview owners won a bitter, five-year struggle with the neighborhood association. The battle went all the way to the Court of Special Appeals which overruled the historic landmark designation established by Baltimore's Commission on Historical and Architectural Preservation. The ruling stood on the premise that government restrictions cannot "deprive the landowner of all reasonable, beneficial use of the property," but did come down with a restriction that limited the change to a parking lot rather than a parking structure. Further screening with trees and plantings produced a more attractive cityscape on a street lined with small, old apartment houses. The curving street with its grassy median and tall trees is quite charming.

With the exception of the 1950 Broadview, construction of apartment houses did not resume until the following decade. A group of garden apartments designed to appeal to retired people, or others who did not want the responsibility of ownership, was built between 1965 and 1967. Located at 4300 North Charles Street, the ninety-one units in eleven buildings are in a secluded area surrounded by trees adjacent to Oak Place. Alexander Porter's Georgian design is simple and straightforward. The Calvert School demolished these apartments and built a middle school.

In the next twenty years, six more apartment houses were built — Highfield House, the Hopkins House, the Cambridge at 3900, the Winthrop, the St. James, and the Colonnade. The Hopkins House, located at the intersection of Linkwood, University Parkway, and 39th Street is in the neighborhood but does not look like part of it. The white masonry construction and the surround of balconies give the impression that it blew in from Miami

Highfield House, 1965, one of six additional apartment buildings in the "golden triangle." (Maryland Historical Society.)

Beach. The location, however, is superb for Hopkins students and staff. These recently constructed apartment houses complete a formidable corridor of prestigious living along Charles Street and University Parkway. It is indeed a "Golden Triangle."

The Cambridge at 3900, dating from 1961 built by Mullan after an uninspired design by Joseph Foust, boasts 234 well-maintained spacious apartments with fine

61

The St. James replaced the Buckingham Arms, destroyed by fire in 1983. (HBF Plus Architects.)

Style of that period. The 165 apartments (now condominiums) occupy fifteen floors. The real estate company brochure stated that the building was "oriented to take fullest advantage of the fascinating panoramic views whose rolling wooded areas are among the loveliest landscape features." Seeing the sunset from one of the upper floors is quite spectacular. The view of the main lobby from Charles Street, with its open glass facade is visually very satisfying. The strongly horizontal character of the building produces a connection with the nearby Canterbury and Cloverhill houses, despite the stylistic differences.

Winthrop House, a dignified condominium of brick construction designed to fit into the scale of the neighborhood, represents a victory for the neighborhood association. The site was under contract for a motor hotel in 1960 until vigorous protests from both Tuscany-Canterbury and Guilford defeated that plan. Parking spaces were built into the design and included with the purchase of a unit. The inclusion of underground, or otherwise hidden, parking space is an admirable aspect of the newer apartments. The Winthrop, with 150 units, was built in 1975, the architect Donald Sickler.

The St. James and the Colonnade both date from 1988. The St. James, designed by HBF Plus Architects, replaced an older apartment building, the Buckingham Arms, lost to fire in 1983. The new building is spare and angular, of dark brick, and different from any of the surrounding buildings. In this respect it is similar to Highfield House and reflects the modernism of thirty years later. The interior is especially well designed without the long corridors, a bane of apartment houses. The Colonnade, for all of its colossal size, has traditional features that relate well to the neighborhood. The brick exterior connects with the

city views appealing to the retired, young professionals, and students. Many have formed a comfortable home in the "Mother Hubbard" building. As with the other Mullan apartments, the parking garage is under a garden surrounding the building.

Highfield House, Mies van der Rohe's modern brick, concrete, and glass building, was first constructed in 1964. Described by well-known Baltimore architectural historian Phoebe Stanton as "simple and elegant," it epitomizes the International

62

row houses behind it and the Hopkins campus in front of it. The pyramidal roof echoes the roof of the Northway. The deep courtyard with its decorated columns softens what would otherwise be an intimidating facade. The "contextual" design is by D'Aleo and Associates.

The Colonnade excited strong neighborhood opposition, partly from its projected size but mainly because plans included a hotel as well as condominiums, shops, and a restaurant that would increase population density and traffic. Despite some design modifications, the building does hold a 125-suite hotel and 120 condominiums. The original restaurant seated 177. The ensemble as a whole is out of keeping with this modest and low-key neighborhood. The Colonnade by its very size calls attention to itself. If it had been set back from the sidewalk and surrounded with grass, small trees, and bushes, there would be a transition from the commercial to the residential buildings. As is, its commercial use is emphasized and one misses the open space and the vegetation that provided a diversion from the sights and sounds of the city.

The predominant building material of Tuscany-Canterbury is brick. Randolph Chalfant, an architect in the neighborhood, describes the various types used in many of our buildings:

The older buildings are built of Baltimore Brick Company's "Homewood Colonial" which was made in their yard at Edison Highway and East Madison Street, now worked out. The Broadview is made from Washington County Brick from Williamsport,

Tuscany-Canterbury

The Colonnade, 1990. (D'Aleo and Associates.)

Maryland. Canterbury Hall is made from Ohio brown brick as are the Tuscany and some others.

When we look around our community, the diversity of buildings—single homes, row homes, apartment houses—some of which we like and some of which we don't, add up to an appealing residential village within the larger city. An article in *The News-American,* February 28, 1981, described the neighborhood as "An Elizabethan city community":

One of Baltimore's oldest and most popular townhouse communities is Canterbury-Tuscany (sic)—north of the Johns Hopkins University campus, between Roland Park and Guilford.

Canterbury-Tuscany is a community that reminds one of Elizabethan times. Its three story houses line such streets as Canterbury, Cloverhill, Tuscany, Highfield and Ridgemede Roads, Tuscany Court and W. 39th and N. Charles Streets . . . [it] is an attractive neighborhood graced by shrubbery and trees that distinguish the townhouses from other neighborhoods. The streets are narrow, and that makes for a quaint appearance and slows down auto traffic. There is no other similar area in the city.

Institutions:
The Calvert School

Part of the "quiet little valley surrounded by high-rises," the Calvert School is located at the corner of Canterbury and Tuscany Roads. The school provides instruction for children from Kindergarten through the eighth grade, and for students worldwide through the Home Instruction Program. Certainly every continent with the exception of Antarctica and virtually every country is supplied with "the School in a Box."

Calvert School was not always located in Tuscany-Canterbury, nor was it always known as Calvert School. In 1897 a small group of physicians, professors, and merchants promoted a "German Kindergarten," based on the educational philosophy of Frederick Froebel, who emphasized motor skills, self-generated activity, and cooperative play. "The Boys' and the Girls' Primary School" was located in cramped quarters above a drug store at the corner of Park Avenue and Madison Street. The curriculum of basic elementary subjects, language, and physical culture lacked a teacher of manual training. Daniel Coit Gilman, then president of the Johns Hopkins University, was instrumental in finding Virgil Hillyer, who soon became the first headmaster. His energy and vision, innovative philosophy of education, and teaching methods led to the Calvert School as we know it today, with its enrollment of close to four hundred students.

By 1900 headmaster Hillyer changed the name of the school to Calvert, the family name of Lord Baltimore. Hillyer also adopted the Calvert colors, black and gold for the school. The little school, then located on Chase Street, outgrew its building by 1918. A move to "the suburbs" appealed to the headmaster and to the board of trustees. Families were moving northward to where the air was clean and fresh, and the transportation was good. The board approved the location, glowingly described by Hillyer, and purchased four lots for $21,000.

Hillyer appointed his friend Lawrence Hall Fowler as architect for the new school, located at 200 40th Street, close to Canterbury Road. The school opened its doors in the autumn of 1924. Unwilling to have the handsome new Calvert School located at so undistinguished an address as 40th Street, Hillyer lobbied to change the street's

Calvert School, 1924.
(Calvert School
Archives.)

name, proposing that it be called Tuscany
Road. Many other street names were hotly
debated. The *Baltimore Sun,* in a December
6, 1927 editorial, urged retention of 40th
Street. Happily, Hillyer prevailed and
honored the Italian countryside he loved
with the Tuscany name. Perhaps Clyde Friz
was similarly moved in that he named two
of his nearby apartments, the Tuscany and
the Lombardy, after Italian districts.

The original Italian-inspired Fowler
building has been expanded three times
since 1924 — in 1972, 1978, and 1986.
One expansion absorbed a Hopkins fraternity house on Canterbury Road, to the
intense satisfaction of the residents of that
street, though there are some who wish that
the Calvert School was not here at all. The
architectural quality of the Calvert school
has suffered from its enlargement. It over-
whelms the space and the hitherto elegant
balance of structure and surround is
compromised. The school purchased two
lots across Tuscany Road, a playing field in

Virgil Hillyer, c.1925.
(Calvert School
Archives.)

65

Calvert School courtyard, c. 1980. (Calvert School Archives.)

1938, and a parking lot in 1986, the latter screened with shrubbery.

The school's interior design is delightful and remarkable. As the children enter, they are in a spacious lobby with the seal from the former Chase Street location underfoot and a handsome chandelier above. Just ahead and up a short flight of steps is a fountain in a blue mosaic grotto with a bronze sculpture entitled "Duck Mother." This endearing sculpture of a small girl with two ducks, goldfish swimming at her feet, is a memorial to a student who died in 1926. The hallways and classrooms are built around five courtyards attractively planted with trees, bushes, and flowers. Something of delight always arrests the eye.

Headmaster Virgil Hillyer and those who came after him "believed in hard work, self-discipline and self-expression through writing." Some aspects of the Calvert system of education have been used in the Baltimore City school system with good results.

The Calvert Home Instruction program was begun in 1905 when a series of epidemics kept children quarantined at home. When these children prospered academically from pursuing class work at home, Hillyer initiated "a scheme for the education of children at home by correspondence." Advertising in *National Geographic Magazine, Scribner's,* and other well-known magazines soon brought more pupils. The program has grown from three thousand in 1920 to more than one hundred thousand from all around the world. The fifty-six-year old Hillyer died of acute appendicitis at Castalia in 1931, preceded by his first wife and infant son. The centennial celebration in 1997 of his school and his work was quite a bash, with a tent covering the entire playing field, and a profusion of golden chrysanthemums everywhere.

Early in the year 2000, Calvert School announced its plans to expand again. This expansion included plans for an equivalent of eighth grade that will add 200 students to the current enrollment and possibly 700 in the future. With the increasing popularity of private school education, Calvert graduates, as well as others, have had difficulty gaining admission to private middle schools. By adding two grades to the curriculum, Calvert hoped to solve that problem. This solution, however, created a serious problem for the Tuscany-Canterbury neighborhood.

In the summer of 2000 the school quietly purchased the house Fowler designed for his sister, at 2 Oak Place, to be used for administrative affairs. A few months later, Calvert's board announced its plans to purchase other property near Oak Place—the eleven luxury apartments at 4300 North Charles Street. By razing the garden apartment buildings (comprising ninety-one units), and purchasing several other fine homes, Calvert acquired space to build a middle school with athletic fields, a gymnasium, and classrooms. Expansion plans also included additions and alterations to the Fowler house, and a parking lot. These plans are by no means a modest expansion. A middle school must meet the criteria for accreditation set forth by the Association of Independent Maryland Schools and by the State Department of Education. It must also have all the resources of other independent middle schools in order to compete successfully in the marketplace. These often include, at a minimum, athletic and gymnasium facilities, library and technology center, science labs, computer labs, language labs, studios for art, dance, and theater, and cafeteria or lunch facilities. Whether Calvert School can continue to fit into a residential community without destroying it as a residential village is questionable. Even with the addition of eight acres to the current five-acre campus, the space will be heavily utilized. The

impact of the middle school development on the surrounding communities will be considerable. While disavowing further expansion to include the high school years, common sense suggests that the Calvert School may become a K–12 institution.

The Scottish Rite Temple of Freemasonry

American architect John Russell Pope, in collaboration with Clyde and Charles Friz, designed the Scottish Rite Temple of Freemasonry on Charles Street. A contemporaneous publication described it as "crown[ing] the upper reaches of Charles Street Avenue . . . in all its Grecian beauty." This classical-style Greek temple, built in 1932, joins the University Baptist Church and the Baltimore Museum of Art in establishing Pope's enduring imprint on the Charles Street corridor. He was also the architect of the much admired Scottish Rite Temple of Freemasonry in Washington, D.C., built in 1915, which probably accounts for his involvement with Baltimore's temple.

While the Scottish Rite Temple looks lonely today, even abandoned, that is not the case. Twice yearly meetings are open to all seven thousand members, only some of whom live in the vicinity. The meetings are held for granting degrees within the organization and take place over an eight-week period. Throughout the year, the Speech and Language Center located in the temple supports treatment facilities for children with aphasia and dyslexia disorders. This program has operated in conjunction with the Maryland Speech and Hearing Agency since 1985. The center provides service for about fifty children, mainly of preschool age. The Speech and Language Center is the principal community outreach and charity of the Scottish Rite Freemasons.

Other branches of freemasonry provide support services for various groups of children with special needs.

First Church of Christ, Scientist

Another neighborhood building, the First Church of Christ, Scientist, designed in the classical style of a Greek temple, is located on University Parkway. The church is one of many branches of the First Church of Christ, Scientist mother church, founded by Mary Baker Eddy in Boston, Massachusetts. In Baltimore the church was first established in the 1890s. The Chapel of the Second Church of Christ, Scientist opened on Christmas Day, 1900, on Mount Royal Avenue and Cathedral Street. The chapel soon united with the First Church. The growing membership needed a new church building. The "Dedicatory Services of First Church of Christ, Scientist, Baltimore, Maryland," recounts this event, " . . . in November 1910 the present location on University Parkway, in what was then a new residential district of Baltimore was

Scottish Rite Temple of Freemasonry, 1932. (Maryland Historical Society.)

purchased. On July 22nd the following year ground was broken and the foundation walls were rapidly built. The corner stone was laid at an early hour in the morning of October 23, 1911, and the church, a beautiful and imposing marble structure with a seating capacity of about 1,000 was dedicated May 25, 1919." The present location, sandwiched between apartment buildings and close to the street with steep steps and a narrow porch, detracts from its impressive appearance. The interior has windows patterned after Tiffany and the architect was Charles Cassell.

The First Church of Christ, Scientist holds regular Sunday services and a Sunday school for children age two or three to twenty. The Reading Room is located in the nearby Rotunda shopping mall.

A woman with close ties to the Church, for all but two of her seventy-six years, relates her experiences as a member with deep emotional satisfaction:

My mother took me to Sunday school from the time I was two, along with my four brothers and sisters. Our next door neighbors belonged to the church, which is how my mother got interested. We lived on Park Heights Avenue then, so my mother had a standing order for two Yellow cabs to take us to the Church every Sunday. We couldn't fit into one cab, but the two cost only twenty-five cents. I guess that was a lot of money then. The Church was filled in those days, even the balcony. You had to go early to get a seat. Now we don't even open the balcony.

I went to Sunday school to age twenty (the customary time of attendance), and then graduated to attend the Church. I joined the Church at age sixteen, which may have been too young to understand everything. I have loved this religion all of my life. The teachers were so wonderful, explaining God and the

First Church of Christ, Scientist, University Parkway   Baltimore, Md.

First Church of Christ Scientist, 1912. (William Hollifield.)

Bible. I knew I was in the right place. There was never a doctor in our house. We always turned to God for answers and we found them.

I married a man who did not belong to the Church, but he took me and our three children every Sunday, and waited for us. After the family grew up, I began to do volunteer work, and I am an usher in the Church. When hard times came into my life, I'd say, "Not my will but thine." That prayer helped me. Prayers always helped me. I say the Daily Prayer every day. "Thy Kingdom come. Let the reign of divine truth, life and love be established in me. Rule out of me all sin, and may thy work enrich the affections of all mankind and govern them."

FOUR

A Neighborhood at Work
1968 to the Present

In Baltimore and elsewhere neighborhood associations sprang up in the late nineteenth century as communities sought to obtain their share of resources and services from the city government. The sense of being treated unfairly or neglected by the city was one of the factors that initiated the formation of these associations, in areas or among groups that already had propinquity, religion, ethnicity, language, or other social characteristics in common. Not surprisingly, community associations developed first in working-class neighborhoods where concern for getting a fair slice of the municipal pie was greatest. In the middle-class suburbs, community associations pressed for services, too, but protection of the community's exclusivity was of paramount importance.

Community associations grew along with the suburbs inhabited by the middle-class and the affluent. The Roland Park Civic League dates from 1891, when that neighborhood was just getting started. The Guilford Association formed in 1939 and the Homeland Association preceded it in 1924. By the time most people bought their homes, neighborhood associations had already been established in these suburban residential areas.

In the case of Roland Park, Edward Bouton created a community, not merely a suburban housing development. It was a propitious time to do so. The middle class was growing, ready for a better life, and the transportation system was there to take them to it. Bouton had the land and provided the

Opposite: Tuscany-Canterbury, May 2003. (Photo by David Prencipe.)

Construction at the Johns Hopkins University, 1922. (Ferdinand Hamburger Archives of the Johns Hopkins University.)

it looks today, yet another fifteen years passed before the sense of community—and the importance of protecting that community—took hold.

The formal process of becoming a community began in 1956. A bound volume of Tuscany-Canterbury Improvement Association minutes spanning a period of a dozen years records how it came about:

The meeting to form an improvement association of Baltimore City residents, in the area roughly bounded on the East by Charles Street, on the North by Warrenton Road [sic] and Cloverhill Road, on the West by Stony Run, and on the South by University Parkway was held in the auditorium of St. David's Church, Oakdale and Roland Avenue, Baltimore, Maryland, on Thursday, March 22, 1956, beginning at 8:15 o'clock P.M.

Mr. Frederic A. Fletcher, acting as chairman, explained how the idea for an organization started and the area that it was to cover, and the purpose of the organization. . . . There was some discussion about . . . whether to call the proposed improvement association "Tuscany-Canterbury Improvement Association" or "University Circle Improvement Association." When put to a vote, the [former] motion was carried.

winding roads and country atmo-sphere, the upscale single-family houses, a country club and women's club, schools, and a shopping mall. He even provided a magazine, *Gardens, Homes and People,* to tell the newcomers how to live in the suburbs. The residents developed a sense of community, not from the sense of being short-changed but from the desire to protect their neighborhoods from untoward development.

A community association came late to Tuscany-Canterbury. The neighborhood developed quite differently from the immediate surrounding neighborhoods. People moved into the University Homes real estate development without much of an idea of how the surrounding area would develop. The great mansions on Charles Street Avenue were still there and eight or ten apartment houses had been constructed. The row houses were convenient and affordable, close to transportation and thus attractive to future homeowners. The 1937 Sanborn map shows the area very much as

At the initial meeting the proposed by-laws, subsequently adopted, laid out the purpose of the organization. "[Formed for] the authorizing and fostering of ways and means to promote the health, education and general welfare of the community and a special need at the present time of an Association to represent the community before the Zoning Commissioner of Baltimore City and the Planning Commission of Baltimore City." Included in the meeting were representatives of the Guilford Civic League and the Roland Park Civic League, each speaking about the experiences of their communities. Both stressed the importance of an association for addressing zoning problems and restrictions in order to make "an impression on lawmakers." Both advised a "war chest," should litigation occur. The language suggests that these communities were apprehensive about the impact of commercial development, as well as any development that might alter the primarily residential character of the community.

The history of the activities of the Tuscany-Canterbury group in the next several years indicates that they, too, had reason to feel concerned about preventing deterioration, commercialization, and new development not in keeping with a residential area.

Conditions within the community were a source of distress, especially to the residents of Canterbury and Cloverhill. Sewage backup from storm drains, rats, trash and debris in the vacant lots and alleys, inadequate lighting, fire hazards created by the vacant barns on the west side of Charles Street, and fraternity houses concerned residents. A plan to enlarge a nursing home on Stony Run Lane was especially alarming. Many of these concerns raised questions of zoning laws that were frequently invoked but not always effective in solving the problem.

The five fraternities that were, at one time or another, located in the neighborhood were a major source of irritation, and

Aerial view of the Johns Hopkins University and Tuscany-Canterbury, c. 1945. (Ferdinand Hamburger Archives of the Johns Hopkins University.)

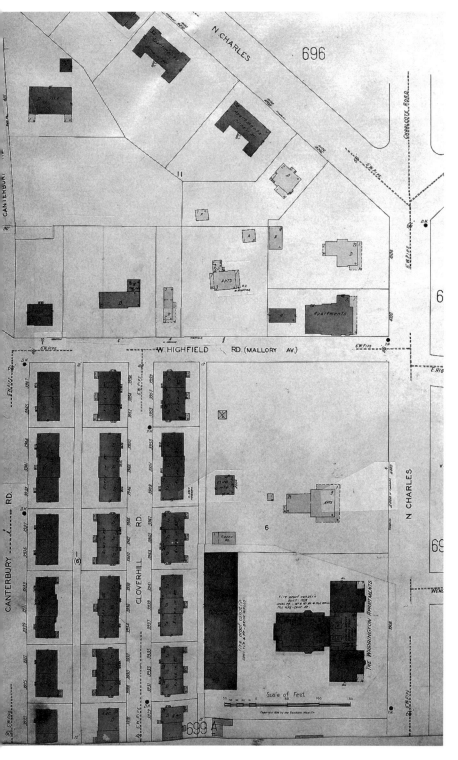

Tuscany-Canterbury on the Sanborn map. (Fire Insurance Maps, 1938/1958.)

Epsilon Pi, Phi Gamma Delta, Phi Sigma Delta and Beta Theta Phi—was probably the most useful intervention. Eventually the fraternities withered away, leaving us now with one, Phi Kappa Psi.

One resident's recollection of life on Canterbury in the heyday of fraternity life is extraordinarily vivid.

I don't know what I can tell you about living here, except that I am very blessed in having such nice neighbors. But I can tell you about the fraternity houses. Now there's only one house, but I remember when there were many, from University Parkway, along Canterbury, on Highfield and on Charles, they could make a loop going from one to another. They were a wild and noisy bunch, creating a lot of distress and disturbance in the neighborhood. While some of the houses were more thoughtful of the neighborhood, most were not inclined to change. And Hopkins wouldn't help at all, telling us they were off campus.

One party was written up in the Sun. I've saved it, but that doesn't really tell everything [Baltimore Sun, June 6, 1972]:

"Latest bacchanalian fraternity party wrecks house and neighbors' nerve"

Imagine if one year they held the NCAA championship lacrosse game in a house instead of a field, with one goal in the upstairs bathroom and the other in the downstairs fireplace. Imagine, in addition, that to keep the players from getting thirsty, they stocked the house with 2,000 gallons of beer. And to keep them from getting lonely, they invited several hundred friends.

You do not have to imagine the end result. To see what happened, all you have to do is to take a look at the Phi Gamma Delta fraternity house, 3908 Canterbury Road, just north of the Johns Hopkins Homewood campus, where last Saturday the boys (15 of whom are members of the Hopkins lacrosse team) had a party. Approaching the house, you pick your

drew complaints about noise and drinking late into the night, trash and garbage, and building disrepair. Neither appeals to the occupants, to the inter-fraternity council, to the university, nor threats of legal action were completely successful. Ongoing dialog with the fraternities—Delta Upsilon, Tau

way through what seems to be the debris of ages: hundreds of empty beer cans, shattered hulks of chairs and sofas, here a rusty vacuum cleaner, there a dismembered washing machine.

You step over what looks like a piano keyboard, briefly noting that every window in the house seems to be broken, and enter the front hall. From the distance comes a faint tinkle of broken glass as the spring wind blows out the last remaining pane.

Appeals to property owners and to various departments in the city government eventually reversed the unsafe, unhealthy, and unsightly conditions, but all took time. The association remained active. For example, in 1968, after a year or more of effort, the city agreed to install "mercury vapor lights" on Canterbury and Cloverhill. Now, some thirty years later, they have been replaced with streetlights that are more appropriate for the ambiance of the neighborhood. Legal intervention was required to block the expansion of the nursing home on Stoneyford Lane from twenty-nine beds to eighty-five. According to the minutes of the Tuscany-Canterbury Association, the home had been illegally in existence for many years. In the first round of intervention, the mayor overrode the association's request, thereby permitting expansion. The minutes of the association do not record the eventual outcome, but we know the plan failed, for now the nursing home is a handsome, two family brick house.

The major cause of concern soon after the association was established, and for the next eight or ten years, was the proposed development of four vacant properties in the neighborhood, three on Charles Street and one on Ridgemede Road. Between 1958 and 1965 plans to develop these properties occupied an enormous amount of the association's energy. Proposals to build on

Colonial Revival house, Stony Run Lane, 1951. (Duane Parroch.)

these lots inevitably raised intense anxiety in the residents of the neighborhood, typical and generally reasonable anxieties regarding the projects' visual impact on the neighborhood, population density, parking, and traffic. Greatest of all was the overarching concern that projects such as these would set a precedent for more development. Each of the properties now has an apartment house, Winthrop House, Highfield House, the Cambridge at 3900, and the Ridgewood. Winthrop House grew out of the community effort to prevent the building of a motor hotel. Several years of protests and threats of litigation finally prevailed, bringing the plan to a halt in 1962. Community concern then shifted to a proposal to build a high-rise apartment building on that site. When zoning was downgraded to permit the high rise, the opposition was so intense that the Tuscany-

Canterbury Association and several individuals entered suit against the mayor and city council of Baltimore for allowing the owners to erect the apartment with parking for 152 families. More than $4,000 was collected to press the suit, but the action was abandoned when the community learned the ultimate cost would be closer to $20,000.

The Ridgewood, located on Ridgemede and opposite the apartment house of the same name, developed from a long and hard-fought, though entirely civilized battle, between the association and the owner, Thomas Mullan of the Mullan Construction Company (who was also a resident member of the association). In 1958, Mr. Mullan proposed a forty-apartment building with thirty parking spaces and two doctor's offices at the Linkwood end of the building. Construction required a change in zoning if the association did not agree to the proposal. After nine years of proposals and counter-proposals, of zoning threats and complaints about the eyesore created by the then-vacant property, the association apparently agreed to thirty apartments and no commercial offices. All of this, despite the warning from a far-sighted board member in 1958, that "Mr. Mullan could sell it and something worse could be put on the lot." During some of these nine years, Mr. Mullan turned his attention to the Cambridge at 3900, where he also confronted community and association objections. In both cases, association objections did result in modifications and improvement of the plans, but the apartment houses were built.

Surprisingly, after numerous successful interventions, the "future of the Association" was brought to the table at a meeting of the board in 1966. The board announced a decision to poll the membership about discontinuing the association.

Although not spelled out, motivating concerns must have included lack of community interest, or perhaps what appeared to be the group's limited impact. The results of the poll were not recorded, but something positive happened, for in 1968, at a special meeting of the board of directors, the acting president, Rear Admiral Valery Havard, recommended a series of proposals to indicate that the association, far from expiring, was alive, well, and rededicating itself. These new objectives included determining the exact boundaries of the neighborhood, notifying the State of Maryland of the new officers in the corporation, collecting dues from the members, establishing committees for neighborhood needs that included traffic, municipal services and zoning, and scheduling a directors' meeting once a month. Letterhead stationery with a logo was already in use. Admiral Havard clearly had exceptional organizational ability in addition to fine character traits. He is described by a neighbor who knew him well as "a very fine man, very concerned about community and people, warm, friendly but with a military bearing."

At the annual association meeting several months later, Havard reported that sewers and storm drains were about to be repaired. Efforts "to keep peace and harmony between college boys and community residents" were also ongoing and "a reasonably satisfactory compromise" had been worked out for 4100 North Charles (the Winthrop). He announced that a liaison had been established with the Northern District Police Station. President Havard then noted that while Tuscany-Canterbury now had over twelve hundred residents, deplorably few were members of the association. He urged all to join, pointing out, "If we don't work to protect ourselves, we will have more objectionable structures, less attention paid to our needs, and the possibility of a decaying neighborhood." His words were prophetic. We have not worked together to protect ourselves (by seeking the protection offered by both national and city preservation organizations), and the residential character of our neighborhood is being eroded (by the expansion of Calvert School).

A geographical unity does not make a neighborhood, but time and leadership does. Our founders started the process, continued the effort and finally produced a viable organization. The major lesson to be learned from the first dozen years relates to property. Property owners cannot be deterred from making use of the land. Owners seek economic gain and the citizenry seeks facilities for living and commerce. That's what cities are all about. Communities, however, can be effective in modifying usage to maintain the integrity of the neighborhood.

A man now approaching middle age tells what it was like to live here, through the years when Tuscany-Canterbury was becoming a neighborhood, and residents banded together to protect it:

My parents settled here in 1956 after my father had his twenty years in the army. It was a great place to grow up. The nice thing about this neighborhood was that it was urban and not Roland Park or Guilford. We had things you wouldn't have further downtown, like Oak Place and Wyman Park and woods and empty fields. We used to go down to Oak Place and crawl in the tunnel where the stream [went underground] all the way to where the Carlyle is now. We did that twice and that was scary. When the old houses on Charles Street were torn down, we were building forts until the apartments were put up.

My father was very protective of the neighborhood and my mother was proud to

Tuscany-Canterbury

May, 2003. (Photo by David Prencipe.)

May, 2003. (Photo by David Prencipe.)

And all those cars? And the parking? The garages on Cloverhill couldn't be used because the driveways were too steep for bigger cars. The association got the apartment houses to put garage space underground. Well, I think the apartment houses defined the neighborhood and protected it. Eventually, my parents thought so, too. When the apartment buildings came to a pause, the neighborhood association was not very active. There was nothing to oppose. All of the buildings were up by the 1970s and also a lot of new people were moving in. When my mother died in 1970 or 1971, my father sold the Cloverhill house and moved out to Lutherville. He was sorry the day he moved and he spent every day after that in Tuscany-Canterbury.

Quiet Years: The Seventies

The 1970s were quiet years. Notes of association meetings, except for one dated June 1978, do not exist. The chief issue raised at that meeting concerned the advisability of membership in the association by occupants of multiple dwellings, such as renters and cooperative or condominium owners. A casual survey of these groups indicated concerns identical with those of homeowners, and the board of directors of the Tuscany-Canterbury Association decided to admit them to membership.

Active Years: The Eighties and Nineties

The 1980s were another matter — a period of vigorous community involvement in the affairs of the neighborhood, especially from the middle of the decade onward. The earliest minutes of the board during this period, dated October 1984, contained a proposal to set aside money to publish a newsletter. A year later, Robert Carter and

live in a row house. My parents were active in the neighborhood association and they opposed every apartment building that was put up, and with good reason. How would the neighborhood work with all those people?

Dennis German, co-presidents of the association, initiated a newsletter to be published twice a year. Unfortunately, we do not have a copy of the first *Tuscany-Canterbury News*. The *News* provided information and also offered a sense of community cohesion, which appears to be ongoing. The first issue in the files of the association is dated August 1985. Earlier ones, if they existed, have been lost to history. That August issue was a "Special Edition" inviting everyone to the "Annual Potluck-Picnic in the Park." The issue also contained an impassioned plea for residents to make known to Mayor William Donald Schaefer their objections to a plan "to give Wyman Park away." The Johns Hopkins University had just proposed to utilize forty acres of the open space for a parking structure and various research buildings. Of even greater concern was the plan to construct "a new clover-leaf entrance road at Linkwood and Stoneyford Roads, passing under the stone bridge into the parkland." That one-page edition epitomizes all that the Tuscany-Canterbury Association is — getting to know your neighbors and protecting the integrity of the neighborhood. Can you imagine what it would be like today to have that cloverleaf entrance on Linkwood Road?

To construct an account of the neighborhood association from 1984 to the present, I have relied upon minutes of the meetings and issues of the newsletter, each of which was a twice-yearly event. Surviving records are incomplete, but they provide enough information to show energetic and determined hard work on the part of the board, together with community support. A reading of these documents strongly suggests that our community would not be what it is today without the work of the board. The introduction of a co-presidency in 1978 was a response to the increasing burden that the business of the association placed on any single individual.

The association functioned, then as now, as watchdog and advocate, thus preventing incongruent development in the neighborhood and lobbying, mainly with the city government, to improve services. Its object was to keep this neighborhood residential for families and homeowners, and for renters who valued living in this pleasant residential area. To this end, a motor hotel, an expanded nursing home, and an assisted living facility were all blocked. New high-rise buildings on the periphery were modified to bring about congruence with the neighborhood. The association regulated their designs, height, number of units, and required off-street parking. It could not prevent inclusion of a hotel in the Colonnade. Despite valiant efforts, commerce won out over community. The same commercial spirit destroyed a Lawrence Hall Fowler house to provide a parking lot for the use of an apartment building constructed in the days before off-street parking was required.

These efforts involved working both with and against the city in enforcing zoning laws. For more than ten years, the association worked with city officials to "down-zone" properties to their existing use and to avoid developing vacant properties (or properties that could become vacant) in ways that would detract from the beauty of the community. On September 2, 1986, Mayor William Donald Schaefer signed into law an ordinance that rezoned the Tuscany-Canterbury area. The law provided for "down-zoning," (restricting use on) seventy properties and thereby reflect and perpetuate current usage and reduce the likelihood of increased density and congestion. This was a victory for the association and the community.

Zoning is a legal measure designed to protect a community from unbridled commercialism. It is not a final protection. As our history illustrates, zoning laws can always be changed. Spot rezoning and variances, or zoning exceptions can and do occur. Obtaining a variance to build a deck is a minor example of the age-old turf war between private and community desires. While a deck does not pose a parking problem, or increase density and congestion, building one does affect neighbors. An alert and informed citizenry, aware of potentially vulnerable areas, is probably the best safeguard for neighborhood integrity. Proactive is generally wiser than reactive. Accordingly, a copy of the zoning map and the zoning laws as they apply to our area is in Appendix 4. Covenants provide additional protection, but this neighborhood has not been supportive of such a plan. Most residents would now agree that omitting the covenants was a shortsighted and excessively self-protective attitude. The neighborhood has no protective regulations beyond zoning laws.

The neighborhood association's advocacy functions include creating helpful liaisons with the city and with nearby institutions and organizations. Working relationships with city agencies brought coordinated street cleaning, trash pick-up and recycling, and increased police effectiveness such as when crime rose in the 1980s and 1990s. Association efforts led to permit parking, to public works assistance in maintaining the median strip and the newly designed rock garden on 39th Street. The group also obtained improvements such as an appropriate fence along the parking lot on 39th Street. The association struggled for twenty-seven months before securing this fence. The city has assisted with tree replacement, and, in 1999, replacing the varied and mostly unattractive street lamps with new and handsome ones. More lights have been requested to finish the project.

The Johns Hopkins University and Loyola College often affect this neighborhood in ways that sometimes arouse concern. Loyola's expansion, a prominent issue in 1986, is no longer a problem. A plan to "adopt-a-park" (Linkwood) as a joint Loyola/Tuscany-Canterbury project may still come to fruition. The improved design of the Hopkins athletic field grew out of community intervention. Tuscany-Canterbury cooperates and works with sister organizations—principally, Greater Homewood and the thirty-five neighborhoods of North Baltimore under its um-

brella—on projects such as the Stony Run clean-up campaign. It works with the Roland Park Civic League to maintain the Stony Run Park and with the Friends of the Roland Park Library to maintain and improve that historic building. Advocacy functions also include internal neighborhood activities. Chief among these is the publication and distribution of the Tuscany-Canterbury News. This quarterly paper is distributed to everyone living in the area, whether or not they are members of the association. All residents are lobbied for membership, and in conjunction with this effort the board produced a complete neighborhood census. The News keeps residents informed of upcoming spring and fall social events as well as important

Tuscany-Canterbury

May, 2003. (Photo by David Prencipe.)

community issues. These issues include crime awareness, new business proposals, signage that does not conform to community standards, changes in the property tax base (with suggested solutions), the possibility of fiber optic cables, the need for traffic sign changes, and pet management (leash and scoop). All of this and more is disseminated through the *News*. The association managed a "first" in the winter of 1999 and hired a commercial company to plow the streets.

The association is tireless in promoting "good neighbor" behavior. In all the records available to me I have found perhaps not more than a half-dozen downright unneighborly acts, not counting the self-willed determination of the strictly commercial enterprises. Each was, in some way, a manifestation of "turf war." In a densely populated neighborhood, with row houses the dominant structures, awareness of the needs of others is especially important. It speaks well for the residents of Tuscany-Canterbury that there have been so few inconsiderate acts. Minutes and accounts of this association's successes and setbacks do not convey the enormous amounts of time and energy that board members have spent promoting and maintaining this neighborhood, a neighborhood loved and enjoyed by so many people. This dedicated group has earned the admiration and respect of the community.

Years of Controversy: 2000 and Beyond

With few exceptions, Tuscany-Canterbury residents and the neighborhood association cooperatively developed and preserved their residential community for almost fifty years. Calvert School's announcement of its planned middle school addition produced an explosive outcry. Immediately and

unexpectedly, the neighborhood and the Neighborhood Association split into rancorous, opposing camps, one group allied in a STOP Calvert campaign and the other in a GO Calvert support of the expansion. Enmity, distrust, and ill will escalated when the Neighborhood Association leaders failed to exert a moderating role. This came about because the president's vigorous support of GO Calvert implied that he represented the board and the neighborhood. The majority of the residents, however, opposed the expansion. The consequence of the president's stand exposed and ignited the quietly simmering discontent with how the Calvert School affected the community.

The community versus school tensions began in 1986 when Calvert extended its first building to the corner of Canterbury Road. Residents of the adjacent row homes complained that school officials showed little regard for them during the construction process. The unanticipated and unannounced destruction of a house across the street from the school slated for a parking lot was a visual negative on Tuscany Road.

It was school traffic, however, that became the major source of frustration and hostility during the nineties. At least 60 percent of the children and the staff lived in the county, and only a few of the city dwellers within walking distance. Consequently, automobiles (increasingly longer and wider ones) backed up for many blocks dropping off and picking up Calvert students. Drivers were all too often unresponsive to the convenience and safety needs of the residents. This callous invasion of our narrow and winding streets inflamed many. One vented her exasperation at a neighborhood meeting:

You have assembled a most intrepid group of wannabe NASCAR drivers, clinging doggedly

*to their right to drive, alone, in a SUV to
deliver one tot, swinging rapidly through the
narrow streets of a very small residential
neighborhood as if it were Daytona Beach. . . .
I invite you to watch on some icy morning
these parents trying to negotiate the hill on
Tuscany Road. Here, perhaps, the Grand Prix
comes to mind. SUVs which work not at all
on ice, slithering backwards, in order to be
gunned with great gusto, and no expertise, up
the hill again. And again.*

The tenants of the 4300 garden apartments acted at once against the sale that
would displace them from the homes in
which many were spending their retirement
years. In broadsides to the community, they
urged cooperative efforts to preserve the
neighborhood, the historic buildings, the
natural environment, and the city tax base
as well as their homes. The 4300 residents
mounted the STOP Calvert campaign,
posted signs and picketed daily in front of
the school. Nonprofits occupied 40 percent
of the tax base and various members of the
city council were concerned about Calvert's
expansion plans. Two bills, 300 and 301,
were introduced by the city council in
which the planning commission would
have to approve demolition of any fifty-plus
residential property units. The 4300 complex has ninety-one apartments. Divided in
its appraisal of the expansion plan, the
association acted slowly. Strong and sometimes bitter debate came out of several
neighborhood meetings, including one with
Calvert School. One of Tuscany-Canterbury's well-known homeowners voiced the
attitude of many residents:

*I am strongly opposed to Calvert School's
expansion into the Tuscany-Canterbury neighborhood. Calvert representative Al Barry was
sent over to my home for "spin control" the
same day the tenants at 4300 were informed*

*they had to move. The first thing I asked
[him] was, "Will the wooded area at the end
of Canterbury Road be touched"? And he said,
"No." Later the plans for Calvert were
unveiled, and I learned this was not the truth.*

*I am a graduate of Calvert School, but I do
not want to live in it. The proposed athletic
fields will be a major disruption to our lives.
I don't want to hear the crowds of people
(mostly county residents who don't pay
Baltimore City taxes) yelling, "Go, Calvert,
go!" anytime of the week. I don't want to
listen to the endless noise of construction or
put up with sports [and] traffic problems any
more than Calvert would like me to show my
most notorious films to its student body each
morning out in front of the school.*

Many residents did not trust Calvert's
described expansion plans or their plans for
the school's future, now a middle school,
when a high school? This mood intensified
even after a general neighborhood meeting
at which residents voted to oppose expansion. Fear of what could happen to the
property if Calvert moved from the community—Loyola dormitories, nursing
home, drug rehabilitation center, or other
commercial enterprises—concerned many
residents.

Some residents wanted the Calvert
School to stay in the neighborhood because
of its value as an educational institution
that attracted tax-paying residents to
Baltimore City. One writer summarized this
position in a letter to *The Sun* on December
27, 2000:

*Calvert School's campus plan is quite sensitive
to its surrounding neighborhoods. It will offer
more green space in full compliance with
environmental regulations . . . the bucolic
4300 property is currently zoned for high
density housing. . . . Were the property sold to
a commercial developer . . . more large-scale*

Tuscany-Canterbury

*Picketing Calvert
School, 2000.*
(Baltimore Sun.)

*apartments or commercial spaces could
forever deface the neighborhood.*

*Opposition to Calvert's low impact over-
looks the many positive contributions of
Calvert School to city life over the past 100
years, the continued need for educational
alternatives to keep tax-paying property
owners and young families in the city and
the many salutary contributions to the
surrounding neighborhoods that Calvert
would bring.*

When the participants at the November
11 meeting voted overwhelmingly to
oppose expansion, the board appointed a
Calvert School Expansion Committee. The
committee proved to be the voice of reason.

They provided facts, allayed fears, dimin-
ished hostility, and fostered objectivity.
They were, however, unsuccessful in their
efforts to meet with Calvert School officials.
The committee encouraged residents to
write letters to city and state representatives
and to attend the city council hearing on
bills 300 and 301. When Mayor Martin
O'Malley indicated he would not sign the
bills, if passed, and when parallel bills in
the State Legislature (House Bill 844 and
Senate Bill 794) were withdrawn in March,
2001, opposition to Calvert's expansion
essentially collapsed. Calvert, possibly at
O'Malley's suggestion, agreed to pay a
reparation fee of $500 to the residents of
4300 and they began to move.

On May 1, at a general meeting, the Tuscany-Canterbury Neighborhood Association elected a new board. The membership of the association immediately passed a motion charging the board to continue opposing the expansion and enlist the help of the mayor in stopping it. If that failed, the board was to hire an attorney and negotiate an agreement with Calvert that would best serve the interests of the community. Recognizing the futility of further opposition, as the city did not support the community, the board proceeded to negotiate an agreement with Calvert. Attorney Albert Figinski guided the renamed Negotiating Committee whose members met with school representatives for more than two months. Both parties signed the resulting Agreement of Restrictive Covenants on July 21, 2001.

The covenant, to remain in effect for twenty-five years, addressed 1) future expansion and the use of facilities, 2) traffic and parking, 3) design, 4) construction. Of most importance to Tuscany-Canterbury was Calvert's agreement not to build an upper school in the neighborhood, nor purchase additional property (with the exception of Castalia) within or adjacent to the neighborhood without prior approval of the association. School officials also agreed to provide parking space for all full-time employees and to limit enrollment to 372 in the lower school and 240 in the middle school. This complex and detailed agreement appears in Appendix 7. John Marchelya, vice-president and lead negotiator for the board concluded that the covenant "made the best of a bad thing."

FIVE

Preserving the Neighborhood
The Twenty-First Century

Our neighborhood did not exist as a separate district until enumerators compiled the 1970 census data. Only three decades of statistics are available. The population of Tuscany-Canterbury hovers today around three thousand. Census takers counted 3,370 persons in 1970 and 2,868 in 1990. We are a predominantly white population. Of those over the age of twenty-five, 67 percent are college educated, as contrasted to 47 percent in 1970. Of those in the work force, employment is mainly professional or technical, 98 percent in 1990, 90 percent in 1980 and 86 percent in 1970. The number of women in the work force increased, from 45 percent in 1980 to 50 percent in 1990. The median income, per person, was $34,764 (per family, $62,321) in 1990,

having almost doubled every decade since 1970. The value of owner-occupied houses followed the same trend, doubling or better every decade.

Of the 2,284 housing units in 1990, 554, or 24 percent were owner-occupied. Home ownership has increased every decade, from 9.2 percent in 1970 to 19.6 percent in 1980. The bulk of the population in the twenty years surveyed were renters, not surprising in view of the number of large apartment houses and the clientele of students and young professionals. The average rental in 1970 was $193, in 1980 it was $309, and in 1990 it was $595. In 1990, there were 521 family households, but only ninety-seven had children.

The number of people between twenty-

May, 2003. (Photo by David Prencipe.)

Guilford Gateway, 1920. (Maryland Historical Society.)

five and sixty-five has declined slightly — 1517, 1597, and 1427 for 1970, 1980, and 1990, respectively. In 1970 there were 1,381 people over age sixty-five, with a slight decline to 1,109 in 1980. A modest but further decline to 883 appeared by 1990. Clearly, residents are inclined to stay in the community. More significantly, the neighborhood is essentially stable, in contrast to the major population trends in the city.

If we remember the remark attributed to Mark Twain that there are lies, goddamned lies, and then there are statistics, these figures reflect as close to statistical truth as one can obtain, given the problems inherent in the data such as missed households or individuals counted twice. In summary, Tuscany-Canterbury is predominantly white, college educated, with professional or technical employment, with incomes in the top 25 percent of the population at large, living in highly desirable homes but not grand residences, whether owner-

occupied or rented. Half of the women are employed. As of 1990 there were very few young children in the neighborhood, but casual observation suggests there are many more today.

The results of the census for 2000 have not yet been analyzed for the various neighborhoods in Baltimore City, and will be only if the city allots money for this project. With libraries closing, crime and grime rampant, schools and education in shambles and the population declining, it is unlikely that the money will be made available. Since North Baltimore neighborhoods tend to remain stable over the decades, the only changes one might find are increasing real estate prices and more young children among the residents.

By any standard, Tuscany-Canterbury is a successful neighborhood. It is attractive, maintains stable property values, offers varied and appealing housing styles, and houses residents who are generally thoughtful of each other and of the community. How does a neighborhood become a place where people like to stay for decades, and where time appears to stand still? The answers are easy to elucidate but more difficult to put into practice. The necessary qualities fall into two categories, those that are external to the community, and those that derive from the residents. The built environment and the social environment both have an impact on the success or failure of a community.

With respect to the built environment, two basic factors stand out—the quality of the housing and its location with regard to the surrounding region. Well-designed and constructed houses are essential. Design is crucial. Houses in the community must follow a design that is a "machine for living," as Philip Johnson, the prominent New York architect, defines it. Typically, the design is the vision of an architect, not a builder. Tuscany-Canterbury is fortunate in that architects rather than builders designed all of the houses. We see attractive and sturdy buildings on every one of our streets. They give the environment strength, permanence, and beauty. Almost all of this community was constructed at a time when building standards were uniformly high. For the most part, they are "pre-war" buildings, a designation which in New York City denotes quality of design and materials. Read again the description of the Warrington, a New York-style apartment house.

Location within the larger area is a second basic quality, one that is mostly beyond the control of a neighborhood's residents but not completely beyond that of the builder. That Tuscany-Canterbury grew in this small ninety-five-acre triangle of the city is an entirely serendipitous happenstance. The major thoroughfares form the boundaries of the community. Unless it has reason to be in the neighborhood, the world passes by Tuscany-Canterbury. That world once passed in horse and buggy equipages, later in streetcars and trains, now in automobiles and buses. The one exception to the boundary streets carrying though-traffic is 39th Street, where the intrusion is minimal. More than street placement gives Tuscany-Canterbury an advantage. The presence of the surrounding, buffer communities — Guilford, Roland Park, Keswick, and the university protect this neighborhood.

Guidelines, covenants, restrictions — these words threaten and alarm many people. They can represent a curb on individual freedom and liberty. Some may view these rules as the antithesis of private property and may seem to be un-American. But are they? We all live within some degree of social restriction. When we experience an infringement on our personal status, many of us rush off to the city, the zoning board, the law, and the courts. We try to invoke our "rights," which is only to say we rush to invoke societal guidelines, covenants, and restrictions. The capacity to sacrifice individual needs for the needs of the community has been a guiding ethic throughout much of American history. Communities will thrive and survive so long as a community spirit prevails.

Considered from this perspective, why are we threatened by guidelines that we, as a community, as neighbors, agree are useful for our neighborhood? Such guidelines protect us from forces originating outside the neighborhood, and from each other. Of course, we all know that ultimate protection does not exist, but covenants and designation as a historic place or district does provide some protection, as well as benefit. There is much to be said for civic pride and for the satisfaction that comes from living in an area that has the status of a historic place, worthy of protection.

The Federal government and Baltimore City both have an interest in preserving our historical and cultural heritage. To appreciate the significance and value of recognition as a historic place or district, both federal and city programs must be understood. The Maryland Historical Trust administers the National Register of Historic Places for this state. The Baltimore City Commission for Historical and Architectural Preservation administers the city program.

At the federal level, the impetus to recognize the historical and cultural heritage of the country began in 1935 with the Historic Sites Act, and was extended in 1966 with the National Historic Preservation Act. As of November 2003 there were 231 sites in Baltimore City listed in the National Register; twenty-three of these are historic districts. Roland Park, Charles Village and Original Northwood are examples of historic districts, and Homewood House of a historic place.

There is a financial benefit to historic designation such as a 25 percent federal income tax credit for "certified historic rehabilitation" when the total cost is $5,000 or more in a twenty-four-month period.

At the city level, preservation of significant buildings and communities began in 1964 with the establishment of the Commission for Historical and Architectural Preservation, known as CHAP. The commission now oversees eighty-two local landmarks and forty-seven historic districts, comprising approximately twenty-five thousand properties. Of especial significance for our community is one of CHAP's main functions, "to review plans for demolition, new construction and exterior changes . . . within local historic districts." That level of oversight could have been enormously beneficial during the Calvert School controversy.

Of benefit also are city property tax credits and state income tax credits for designated properties. For single-family residences, the cost of replacing a slate roof and windows could exceed the minimum amount qualifying an owner for a tax credit. For apartment houses or other public buildings, the value of tax credits is evident. The Northway would be unable to obtain any tax credits for that rehabilitation project if it were not in a historic district. Tax credits can also be transferred to a mortgage holder, thus reducing the mortgage. Finally, property taxes can be frozen at the pre-rehabilitation level for ten years.

It is important to note that neither type of historic designation mandates repairs or renovations, nor is the use or sale of the property restricted. Only local zoning laws restrict what can be done to or with a property.

The idea of covenants and of inclusion as a historic place or district, under National Register guidelines, was vetoed by this community in 1990. Ten years later, with surrounding communities already on the National Register, or seeking to be, various residents and former residents promoted the value of our neighborhood seeking to become a historic district. To qualify for inclusion on the National Register, a place or district must meet the following criteria. It must be more than 50 years of age, be distinctive in design, setting, materials or workmanship, and express a major trend in the history of the community, the city, and the nation. Tuscany-Canterbury certainly meets these criteria.

The effort to interest residents in this project culminated at the semi-annual neighborhood meeting on June 14, 2000. Jill Storms, an architect and former resident, and Peter Kurtze, of the Maryland Historical Trust, explained the purpose, meaning, and significance of becoming a historic district. The prevailing attitude that designation as a historic district would interfere with personal property rights was largely dispelled. The advantages were spelled out and included, first, the symbolic advantage of knowing the community was a special place worth preserving. Second, historic status would maintain neighborhood stability and property values and third, the federal, state, and city tax advantage for repairs, replacement, and renovation costs in excess of $5000.

The two speakers also compared National Register designation with the Commission for Historical and Architectural Preservation operated by Baltimore City. The latter is more restrictive regarding property alteration and thereby offers more historic status protection. CHAP guidelines also require more than half of the property owners to endorse the request to join the existing forty-seven historic districts in the city. The main focus of the meeting was to develop a favorable interest in being included on the National Register, and that was accomplished.

At its November meeting, the board of the Neighborhood Association voted to seek historic designation and to contribute $1000 to prepare the application. Two problems had to be solved, additional funding and the services of a knowledgeable person to do the necessary research and write the application.

Funding could be obtained from the residents, neighborhood businesses, or a private source. Preservation Maryland, a statewide organization devoted to preserving Maryland's historical heritage through advocacy, education, and funding was a suitable and logical prospect. The text of the application stated:

Tuscany-Canterbury is a primarily residential, North Baltimore neighborhood, built mainly between World War I and World War II, comprised of picturesque Colonial and Tudor style row homes, exclusive apartment houses and three institutional buildings. Constructed on the site of the Cloverhill farm, part of the land grant to the Merryman family from Charles, Lord Baltimore in 1688, it was developed by George Morris, Clyde Friz and Thomas Mullan. Architects significant in its history include John Ahlers, Lawrence Hall Fowler, John Russell Pope and L. Mies van der Rohe. The naturalistic landscape follows the principles espoused by Frederick Law Olmsted.

The built environment serves established professional families as well as young professionals and students from Johns Hopkins University in the apartment dwellings. The neighborhood itself is noted for stability, quality of environment and location adjacent to academic, religious, medical and cultural facilities.

Dean Wagner undertook the research and writing. He had extensive experience in working with National Register applica-

Frederick Law Olmsted, by John Singer Sargent (Biltmore Estate, Asheville, North Carolina.)

tions in Maryland, Pennsylvania, New York, and Ohio. His research skills and his knowledge of the built environment enabled him to meet the February 1, 2001 deadline with the expectation of a favorable action within the calendar year.

The Maryland Historical Trust approved the application, and with praise for its quality, sent it to the Baltimore City Planning Commission and Commission for Historical and Architectural Preservation (CHAP). Both CHAP and Mayor Martin O'Malley endorsed the application on May 8, 2001. The Governor's Consulting Committee acted favorably on the application and the various endorsements on May 22, 2001. The National Park Service maintains the National Register and provides the official listing within several months.

The trajectory from open, country land to a historically significant community took place in a time span of 100 years.

Even without designation as a historic place or district, covenants provide considerable protection. The guidelines utilized by the Roland Park Roads and Maintenance Corporation, for example, are simple, clear, and straightforward directives. Roland Park residents do not find the restrictions burdensome, and, according to real estate news, covenants are one of the reasons for Roland Park's strong property values.

Although Tuscany-Canterbury does not have covenants there have been few unfortunate changes in the front facades of the houses, which suggests that most residents are protective of the neighborhood's architectural integrity. Years ago, one resident did enclose the entire front porch and was required to remove it. Another example, barely visible from the street, concerns painting the facade. A gable at the end of a group is painted glaring white, including the half-timbering. The rest of the group retains the Tudor style.

More recently, a resident on Tuscany Road planned a porch enclosure out of keeping with the architecture but modified it as a result of neighborhood pressure. Another resident of Tuscany Road changed the third floor window from a tiny casement to a modest, double-hung window to admit more light to the room. One neighbor pointed out the incongruity of the exterior trim and the householder modified the design at a considerable extra expense. Roofing material is another issue. Some residents object to the cost of slate replacements. Fortunately, there are more reasonable alternatives, specifically high-quality fiberglass shingles in an appropriate color.

Changes to the rear of the buildings, mainly the addition of decks, have caused the most consternation, and in some cases, litigation, usually to no avail. Even though there are very specific zoning regulations about additions to the rear, an application for a variance tends to be acted upon favorably by the zoning board on the ground that similar structures already exist. The interference with privacy and light, often an issue, is not considered by the zoning board. Deck fever seems to have struck in the late 1970s, and it goes on. There are now about fifty-four decks in the neighborhood.

The architectural guidelines recommended by the Tuscany-Canterbury neighborhood association are included in Appendix 3. Following these guidelines will deter what one angry resident referred to as the "Do-as-I-damn-please Mode of Urban Development." To avert any further destruction of the neighborhood, the Tuscany-Canterbury Neighborhood Association should request inclusion as a historic district under the auspices of the Committee on Historical and Architectural Preservation in Baltimore City. The association should also develop covenants, and educate our residents and our institutions about the value of preservation.

Tuscany-Canterbury

Appendix A

Guide to Architects and Buildings

Lawrence Hall Fowler

10 West Highfield Road, French Eclectic

105 Tuscany Road (Calvert School), French Eclectic

200 Tuscany Road (Castalia), Tudor Revival

2 Oak Place (Calvert School Extension), Georgian Revival

John A. Ahlers

213–215 Tuscany Road rowhomes, Half-Timbered Tudor

301–313 Tuscany Road rowhomes, Half-Timbered Tudor

323–333 Tuscany Road rowhomes, Half-Timbered Tudor

Cyril Hebrank

315–321 Tuscany Road rowhomes, Half-Timbered Tudor

Kenneth Cameron Miller

4202–4213 Tuscany Court rowhomes, Half-Timbered Tudor, Federal Revival

Edward H. Glidden Sr.

100 West 39th Street (Canterbury Hall), Half-Timbered Tudor Revival

101 and 103 West 39th Street, (The Hamilton and The Hamlyn), Georgian Revival

Wyatt and Nolting

100 West University Parkway, Georgian Revival

3908 North Charles Street, (The Warrington), Georgian Revival

Ludwig Mies van der Rohe

4000 North Charles Street, (Highfield House), International Style

John Russell Pope with Clyde Friz

220 Stony Run Lane, (the Lombardy), Italian Renaissance

221 Stony Run Lane, (the Tuscany), Italian Renaissance

230 Stony Run Lane, (the Gardens of Guilford),

4201 Linkwood Road, Tudor Revival

3800 North Charles Street, (Scottish Rite Temple of Freemasonry), Neoclassical Style

George R. Morris

Rowhomes on Canterbury and Cloverhill English Style

93

Appendix B

Architectural Guidelines

Purpose

Tuscany Canterbury is an architecturally rich and diverse Baltimore community. Therefore, it is suggested that the community endeavor to institute a set of guidelines to preserve its architectural heritage and its property values. Guidelines serve two purposes: to educate the residents about alterations which will enhance property values, or alternatively, detract from property values and to establish a consistent level of expectations as a basis for enforcement of standards.

Recommendations

With the variety of home styles, of property locations relative to surrounding property, and the visibility of exterior alterations or changes, it is essential that each proposed change be reviewed by a Standing Committee, appointed by the Board of the Tuscany Canterbury Neighborhood Association, comprised of community residents, including one architect, or an outside consulting architect. This Committee is to be considered as an advisory body, except for issues of zoning.

Guidelines

One: Consistency within groupings of homes. Most of the town house groupings were designed as a unit. Continuity of architectural features, roofing materials, and paint colors should reflect this unity.

Two: Additions and alterations. Proposed additions can, by their very nature, affect the unity of a group. The visibility and context of proposed alterations or additions are factors to be considered. It is recommended that any changes visible from the street should be consistent with the existing structure, and the specific surroundings. Issues of individuality, creativity and affordability should also be considered. Greater latitude can be permitted to changes at the rear of buildings. A ramp for a handicapped resident is acceptable.

The specific recommended guidelines are as follows:

1. ROOFS: Slate or slate substitute, such as Supra Slate or Supradur, is required. Consistency within units of homes must be maintained. If the cost of reconstruction with slate is prohibitive, consensus of the residents within the grouping, must be obtained. Television antennae should be removed when cable is connected.

2. SHUTTERS: Shutters should be compatible in style and color with others in the grouping of houses and in the neighborhood.

3. PAINT: Paint color should be consistent within the grouping. The Committee should be consulted about variations.

4. GUTTERS AND DOWNSPOUTS: Consistency within the grouping is strongly recommended.

5. GARAGE DOORS AND PARKING AREAS: Sliding or overhead garage doors with a traditional appearance are acceptable. Parking areas must be paved with concrete, brick, or flagstone. Carports are not permitted. Appropriate landscaping is recommended.

6. OUTSIDE LIGHTING: The lighting should be for pathways or for the building. Lighting should not shine on the neighboring property or on public areas.

7. HEATING AND COOLING EQUIPMENT: Units for air conditioning and heat pumps should send the noise skyward, not at adjoining homes. Placement should not be near a neighbor's residence.

8. ALARM SYSTEMS: Any unobtrusive system is acceptable. The alarm should sound inside the house; outside sound boxes are not permitted unless several adjacent residents have access to turn off the alarm. Placing the advertising sign of the alarm system in front of the house is discouraged.

9. YARD ENCLOSURES AND FURNISHINGS: Front fences are not permitted; hedges should be limited to four feet in height. Rear fences or hedges should also be limited to four feet in height. Landscaping with natural materials, mailboxes, and house number signs, are the only acceptable front yard furnishings. Holiday decorations are permissible.

10. ADDITIONS, DECKS, AND PATIOS: Detailed drawings indicating dimensions, materials, colors and site plan must accompany applications to the Committee for consideration. The scale and style of the change or alteration must harmonize with the existing structure, the adjacent structures, and be in keeping with the ambience of the neighborhood.

11. SIDEWALKS: Sidewalk replacement should conform to existing sidewalks. The pebble style is the neighborhood standard.

12. RESTORATION: Materials, colors and designs should conform with, or be compatible with the original architecture and construction of the building to be restored. Sources of compatible material can be obtained from the Tuscany-Canterbury Neighborhood Association.

A. J. O'Brien 2000

Appendix C

Tuscany-Canterbury Association By-Laws

Article I: Name and Purpose

Section 1. Recognizing the need for representation in their community, particularly in the authorizing and fostering of ways and means to promote the health, education, safety and general welfare of the community and a special need at the present time of an Association to represent the community before the Zoning Commission of Baltimore City and the Planning Commission of Baltimore City, the residents of Baltimore City in the area roughly bound on the East by Charles Street, on the North by Warrenton Road and Overhill Road, on the West by Stony Run, and on the South by University Parkway have associated themselves together for the purpose of promoting by legitimate means the foregoing and approved objectives; the association is to be nonpolitical and non-sectarian having for its one objective the development and general welfare of this particular section of the City of Baltimore. This Association shall be operated exclusively for local improvement, educational, charitable and other non-profitable purposes.

Article II: Members

Section 1. Members of the Association shall be those persons who signify their intention to become members of the Association and who shall therefore pay the proper dues and who are residents or property owners of the covered area and are at least eighteen years of age.

Article III: Board of Directors

Section 1. The Board of Directors shall consist of twelve members and the officers. Each Director shall reside within the boundaries of the Association and shall be a member in good standing. Each Director shall serve for a one year term and may succeed him/herself, except for the term of Second Vice President, First Vice President, and President as provided in Article IV, or until his/her successor is elected and qualified.

Article IV: Officers

Section 1. The officers of the Association shall consist of a Second Vice President, a First Vice President, a President, a Recording Secretary, a Corresponding Secretary, and a Treasurer/Membership

Officer. Each shall be chosen by the membership at the annual meeting. The Second Vice President, First Vice President, and President, shall serve one-year terms. The terms shall be overlapped in order that every year the Second Vice President's, First Vice President's, and President's terms shall expire. Annually, the Second Vice President will matriculate to the position of the First Vice President, and the First Vice President will matriculate to the position of President. An annual election will be held for the position of Second Vice President.

Election

Section 1. The Second Vice President, First Vice President, President, Secretaries, and all members of the Board of Directors shall be elected by the members present at the Spring meeting. Except at that meeting, nominations for the Board of Directors shall be made by a nominating committee appointed by the Second Vice President, First Vice President, and President, thirty days prior to the Spring meeting and named in the notice of that meeting. Additionally, nominations of persons present and accepting may be made from the floor at that meeting and election shall be by ballot by those members present.

Article V: Meetings

Section 1. Semiannual meetings shall be held in the Spring and the Fall of each and every year with the specific date and place set by the Board of Directors. Notice shall be delivered to the membership at least fifteen days prior to the meeting.

Section 2. Special meetings of the Association may be called by the Second Vice President, First Vice President, and President, at any time and shall be called by them upon the written request of the six members of the Board of Directors or twenty-five members of the Association. Notice of the special meeting shall be delivered to the membership by the Secretary not less that five days prior to the special meeting.

Section 3. The Board of Directors shall have at least four meetings in each year. The date, time, and place of the meetings shall be determined by the Board of Directors.

Section 4. Special meetings of the Board of Directors may be called by the Second Vice President, First Vice President, and President at any time and shall be called upon the written request of three members of the Board of Directors. The Corresponding Secretary shall give notice at least twenty-four hours before such meetings to all members of the Board of Directors.

Section 5. All notices of meetings shall include an agenda. Only motions concerning the agenda can be voted upon at meetings.

Section 6. Twenty-five percent of the members of the Association shall constitute a quorum at any semiannual or special meeting of the membership. Only one vote per member present is allowed. Fifty percent of the eligible Directors shall constitute a quorum at the Board meeting.

Article VI: Dues

Section 1. The dues of the Association shall be set by the Board of Directors. There shall be three classes of membership as follows: individual, family, organizational. Each member is entitled to one vote. In the case of family membership, each family is entitled to two votes. In the case of organizational membership, each organization is entitled to one vote.

Section 2. Dues shall be payable annually in advance of the Spring meeting of the Association, and no member whose dues are unpaid shall be entitled to vote at any meeting of the Association or Board of Directors.

Section 3. The fiscal year shall begin on February 1 and end on January 31 or as set by the Board of Directors.

Duties of Officers

Section 1. The Second Vice President, First Vice President, and President shall preside at all meetings of the Association. They shall submit a written report to the membership at the Spring meeting, covering the activities of the Association during the past fiscal year. They shall appoint all committees, and shall require committee reports from time to time for use in the annual report. They may call a special meeting of the Association. They shall have such other powers as are usually exercised by the office or other such powers and duties as granted by the Board of Directors.

Section 2. The Recording Secretary shall keep an accurate record of all meetings of the Association or the Board. The Corresponding Secretary shall conduct all routine correspondence and other communications authorized by the Second Vice President, First Vice President, President, and the Board or the Association and shall keep records thereof. He or she keeps a list of the membership and shall give notice to the members of all meetings as required herein. He or she shall, within thirty days after the Spring meeting mail to the membership a report of the proceedings of said meeting, listing new board members and the names

of the officers elected for the ensuing year, together with copies of the Second Vice President's, First Vice President's, President's, and the Treasurer's report.

Section 3. The Treasurer shall collect all monies due the Association and deposit them in a bank to be selected by the Treasurer. Funds of the Association shall be paid out only on checks signed by any two of the following: the First Vice President, the President, the Treasurer. The Treasurer shall furnish to the Corresponding Secretary from time to time a list of the members in good standing. He or she shall submit such reports from time to time as may be directed by the Second Vice President, First Vice President, and President. Prior to the Spring meeting, the Treasurer shall prepare a written report covering the state of the Association's finances.

Article VII: Miscellaneous Provisions

Section 1. No obligation for the payment of funds on behalf of this Association shall be incurred beyond funds in hand.

Section 2. No officer or Director shall be personally libel for any debt incurred by the Association.

Section 3. These By-Laws may be amended at any meeting of the Association by an affirmative vote of two-thirds of the members present and entitled to vote. Any such amendment shall be submitted to the Corresponding Secretary at least thirty days prior to the meeting. Amendments can be submitted by at least fifteen members of the Association or through the Board. The substance of such amendments shall be included by the Secretary in the notice of the meeting at which such amendments are to be acted upon.

Section 4. Any proposed change in existing zoning regulations on any property

within the Tuscany-Canterbury Association area must be voted on by the Board of Directors at a regular or special meeting, before the Association's sanction thereof may be given or publicized. An affirmative vote of two-thirds of the Board of Directors will be necessary. The proposed change shall be clearly set forth in the notice of the meeting. The result of the voting shall be published to the membership within thirty days after such meeting or prior to any public hearing.

Approved April, 2000

Tuscany-Canterbury

Bibliographical Note

Of the many publications that provided information for this book, the major ones are noted here. Others, relating to a specific point, are indicated in the text.

For research on Baltimore, "The Records of a City: Baltimore and Its Historical Sources," by Richard J. Cox and Patricia M. Vanorny [*Maryland Historical Magazine*, 70 (1975): 286–310], is an essential guide. Robert J. Brugger, *Maryland: A Middle Temperament, 1634–1980* (Baltimore: The Johns Hopkins University Press, 1988), a veritable encyclopedia, is an important reference for even so narrow a subject as this one. Three neighborhood histories were especially helpful: Karen Lewand, *North Baltimore: From Estate to Development* (Baltimore City Department of Planning and the University of Baltimore, 1989); James F. Waesche, *Crowning the Gravelly Hill: A History of the Roland Park, Guilford-Homeland District* (Baltimore: Maclay and Associates, 1987); and Sherry Olson, *Baltimore: The Building of an American City* (Baltimore: The Johns Hopkins University Press, 1980). Joseph M. Coale III, *Middling Planters of Ruxton, 1694–1858* (Baltimore: Maryland Historical Society, 1996) proved instructive both as a local history and as a manual for understanding the sequence of land ownership from king to noble to

commoner. Closer to the subject, the Very Reverend John Newton Peabody's *The Cathedral Grounds from the Indians to Today* (Baltimore: Cathedral of the Incarnation, 1976) served as a springboard to learning about the Merryman family and their Clover Hill farm.

Additional details about the Merryman family can be found in Frances B. Culver, "Merryman Family," *Maryland Historical Magazine*, 10 (1915): 176–85, the Diehlman/Hayward file at the Maryland Historical Society Library, the Maryland Room at the Enoch Pratt Library, and Baltimore City and County land records. William Marye's delightful and detailed chronicles of the Merrymans and Clover Hill are in "Baltimore City Place Names, Part 3: Stony Run, Its Plantations, Farms, Country Seats and Mills," *Maryland Historical Magazine*, 58 (1963): 211–32, and Part 4, ibid., 59 (1964): 52–93. Farming practices used in this region, especially by the Carroll family, are discussed in Carville Earle and Ronald Hoffman, "Genteel Erosion: The Ecological Consequences of Capitalist Agriculture in the Chesapeake, 1730–1840," in Philip D. Curtin, Grace S. Brush, and George W. Fisher, eds., *Discovering the Chesapeake: The History of a Watershed Ecosystem* (Baltimore: The Johns

Hopkins Press, 2001). Despite its formidable title this book is easy to read and packed with information about the land and its inhabitants from prehistory to the twentieth century. It's worth a browse. I have used other bits and pieces without giving specific credit.

Several old maps demonstrated the value of pictures, as opposed to words, in describing the topography and what man has done to it. The G. M. Hopkins *Atlas of Baltimore, Maryland and Environs* (Philadelphia: T. Bourquin, 1876–1877) is a treasure and is described in the text. *The City of Baltimore Topographical Survey,* by Thos. M. Ward, July, 1894, is equally instructive, though less picturesque than the Hopkins atlas. *The 1914 Atlas of the City of Baltimore,* published by the Topographical Survey Commission, shows our neighborhood on the eve of what we know today. Diane L. Oswald, *Fire Insurance Maps: Their History and Applications* (College Station, Texas: Lacewing Press, 1997), summarizes the history of the Sanborn maps. Marvels of clarity, the 1935 and 1952 maps depict the neighborhood at two significant periods. Reading the land records conveys the difficulties of delineating property lines in the wilderness with primitive surveying methods.

Accounts of street growth, turnpikes, and various forms of public transportation are scattered in books, articles, newspaper stories, and clippings in library files. Michael R. Farrell, *The History of Baltimore Streetcars* (Sykesville, Md: Greenberg Publishing Company, 1973) is packed with information and a delight for the railroad buff. George W. Hilton, *The Ma and Pa: A History of the Maryland and Pennsylvania Railroad* (Berkeley, Calif.: Howell-North, 1963) is an affectionate story. By contrast is the somber story in William Hollifield, *Difficulties Made Easy: History of the Turnpikes of Baltimore City and County* (Towson, Md.: Baltimore County Historical Society, 1978).

Information about buildings and architects came from a variety of sources. The *Baltimore Sun,* the *Baltimore News-American,* and the *Daily Record,* the Maryland Room of the Enoch Pratt Free Library and the Maryland Historical Society Library, land records in Baltimore City and County, and personal communications. Dean Wagner's willingness to share his file on the elusive John Ahlers filled an otherwise empty spot in my account. Frank Chouteau Brown's "Tendencies in Apartment House Design," *Architectural Record,* 50 (1921): 489–503 featured an interesting account of the Tuscany apartment house. Egon Verheyen, ed., *Laurence Hall Fowler, Architect* (Baltimore: The Johns Hopkins University Press, 1984), is a useful biography and catalog of drawings and commissions for buildings. The quotation from Fowler's correspondence comes from the Fowler documents in Special Collections at Evergreen House.

The history of Calvert School is set forth in Archibald Hart's *Calvert and Hillyer, 1897–1947* (Baltimore: Waverly Press, 1947). Although detailed and informative, it is not a critical assessment of the school's educational philosophy. For understanding the role and purpose of neighborhood associations in the life of a community, and in the city, Joseph L. Arnold, "The Neighborhood and City Hall: The Origin of Neighborhood Associations in Baltimore, 1880–1911," *Journal of Urban History,* 6 (1979), is obligatory reading. Finding it was equivalent to finding the mother lode. The bibliography is a treasure.

Census data can sometimes be obtained from the Baltimore City Department of Planning, otherwise consult your library. The Bureau of the Census Neighborhood Statistics Program provides narrative profiles of neighborhoods. Although interesting, the census data is more useful, especially for making neighborhood comparisons. Data for 1970 and 1980 came from Allan Goodman and Ralph B. Taylor, *Baltimore Neighborhood Fact Book: 1970 and 1980* (Baltimore: The Center for Metropolitan Planning and Research, The Johns Hopkins University, 1980).

Two organizations provide information about historical designation and preservation: Baltimore City Commission for Historical and Architectural Preservation, 601 City Hall, 100 North Holliday Street, Baltimore, Maryland 21202 (410-396-4883); and Maryland Historical Trust, Division of Historical and Cultural Programs, Maryland Department of Housing and Community Development, 100 Community Place, Crownsville, Maryland, 21032-2023 (410-514-7601).

Tuscany-Canterbury

Index

Tuscany-Canterbury

Havard, Valery, Rear Adm., 76–77
Hayfields, 5
Hebrank, Cyil, 43
Highfield House, 21, 36, 54, 61–63, *61*, 75
Highfield Road, 46
Hillyer, Virgil, 64–65, *65*, 66
Homeland, 15
Homeland Association, 71
Homewood, purchase from Carroll family, *14*, 15; built by Charles Carroll, 25
Hopkins House, 60, 61
Hyde family, 11, *16, 21, 22, 26,* 35
Hyde, George Washington, Maj., *17, 32*
Hyde, Ray, *16*

James I (king), 3
Johns Hopkins University, 25, 60, *72, 73,* 79, 81

Lincoln, 51
Linkwood Apartments, 28
Linkwood Road, 10, 38, 49–50
Lombardy, 52
Loyola College, 81

McDonald, William, 14, 27
Mallory, Jeremiah D., 16
Marye, William, 6, 7
Maryland and Pennsylvania Railroad, 28–29, *37*, 50
Maryland Historical Trust, 90, 91
Merryman, Charles, 3, 5, 6, 9; properties, 5, 8, 9
Merryman, John, [1714 land grant], 5, 6, 7, 8, 24
Merryman, John, Cloverhill Farm, Parkton, 5–6
Merryman's Court, 5
Merryman's Lane, 5, 10, 14, 24, *24*, 25, 26
Merryman's Lott, 4, 5
Miller, Kenneth Cameron, 44

Mills, 26–28
Morris, George, 23, 32, 34, 35, 36, 38, 50
Mullan Contracting Company, 40, 43, 56, 57–59, 61
Mullan, Thomas, *41*, 76
National Register of Historic Places, 89
Northway, 21, 57
Northwood, 43

Oak Place, 47–48, *47*, 67
Oakenshawe, 33
O'Brien, Belle, 15, *15*, 24
Olmsted [Frederick Law] firm, 25, 26, 29, *91*
O'Malley, Martin, 84, 92
100 University Parkway West, 55, 56
104 and 106 West, 51

Palmer, Edward L., architect, 51
Paradise Mill, 10, 26, *27*, 28, 49
Parks, 29
Phillips, George T., 18, 19
Phillipshurst, *18*, 19, 21
Pietsch, Theodore Wells, 52
Pope, John Russell, 67–68
Preservation Maryland, 91

Reese, Charles, 3, 9
Ridgemede, 13, 40, 41, *42*, 43, 56, 58
Ridgewood, 59, 75, 76
Robinson & Slagle Company, 40, 43
Roland Park, 11, 25, 71–72, 90
Roland Park Civic League, 71, 73, 81
Roland Park Company, 19, 43
Roulou, Louis, 57

St. James, 21, 62, *62*
Schaeffer, William Donald, 79
Scottish Rite Temple of Freemasonry, 19, 37, 68, *68*
Sickler, Donald, 62
Solter family, 11

Stony Run, 6, 7, *7*, 11, 25, 26, 27, 28, 29, 45, 50
Stony Run Lane, 75

Tollgate, 15, *15*, 23–24, *24*, 26
Tudor Arms, 25
Tuscany Apartments, 50, 52, *52*
Tuscany-Canterbury neighborhood, 3, 11, *35*, 51, 66, *70, 81*; apartment buildings, 50–54; architecture of, 31–35, 37, 38, *38*, 46–52, 63–64, 88–89, 92; boundaries of, 13–14; 18, 26, 29, *30, 35*, 58, *58*; on community guidelines and restrictions, 89–90, 92; flora, 52–54; fraternities, 73–75, *74*; gas lighting, 39, historic designation, 89–90; neighborhood association activities, 71–85, *73, 84*; neighborhood newsletter, 78–79, *80, 81*; oldest house, *44*, 45; population, 87–88; street lighting, 39, 75, 80–81; *77, 86*; tax credits, 90; prior to World War II, 54–59; post World War II, 60–64; zoning issues, 79–80, 92
Tuscany Court, *40*, 43–44
Tuscany Road, 40, 41–43, 46, 50

University Homes, 18, *32*, 36; architectural styles of, 34–35; company formed 32; land restrictions, 33; and natural gas heating, 36, *36*, 72
University Parkway, 5, 23–24, *24*, 24–25, 26
University Parkway Company, 13, 52
University Parkway Pharmacy, 56

Warrington, 21, *21*, 38, 54
Winthrop House, 21, 45, 54, 61, 75–76
Woodcliff Manor, 60
Wyatt and Nolting, 54, 55
Wynnewood Towers, 29